A Modest Genius

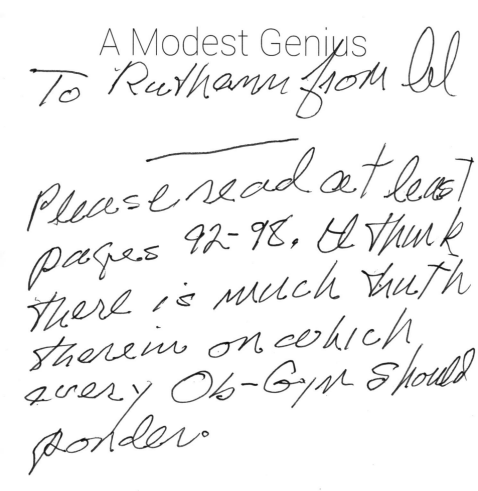

To Ruthann from Bill

Please read at least pages 92-98. I think there is much truth therein on which every Ob-Gyn should ponder.

A Modest Genius

The story of Darwin's Life and how his ideas changed everything

Hanne Strager
Foreword by Sarah Darwin

Copyright © 2016 Hanne Strager

Cover Design © 2016 Alette Bertelsen

English translation Graham Timmins, *http://www.therightword.info*

ISBN: 1517714338
ISBN 13: 9781517714338

In memory of my parents

Foreword

"The day has passed delightfully: delight is however a weak term for such transports of pleasure: I have been wandering by myself in a Brazilian forest. . . . A most paradoxical mixture of sound & silence pervades the shady parts of the wood, —the noise from the insects is so loud that in the evening it can be heard even in a vessel anchored several hundred yards from the shore. —Yet within the recesses of the forest when in the midst of it a universal stillnes appears to reign. —To a person fond of natural history such a day as this brings with it pleasure more acute than he ever may again experience."[1]

I AM OFTEN asked what I think Darwin would be most interested in if he were alive today. I am sure he would be excited to learn about the discovery of DNA, which as the mechanism for inheritance undoubtedly supports his theory of evolution. I think Darwin would also be a fervent supporter of nature conservation, perhaps not by chaining himself to bulldozers or living in trees—after all, he was a modest and private man. But I know that Darwin would continue to communicate the wonders of the natural world to as wide an audience as possible—much as he did during his nineteenth-century lifetime.

---

1   Keynes, R.D., ed. 2001. *Charles Darwin's* Beagle *Diary*. Cambridge: Cambridge University Press.

Darwin wrote *On the Origin of Species* for a wide audience, not for the specialist reader. Indeed, it was even for sale at railway stations and sold out on the day of publication. Nowadays, you'll likely find a copy of this book on the shelf in many households, perhaps quite dusty and maybe not read by so wide an audience as when it was first published. Hanne Strager's marvellous book brings us an engaging summary of Darwin's work, weaving together stories and glimpses from his private life and his discoveries with more recent developments in science and conservation. *A Modest Genius* provides a contemporary perspective on Darwin's work that helps us understand our place on the planet.

Darwin realized that humans were part of the animal kingdom and indeed suggested a common origin of all living things; this is now supported by contemporary research. Today one should consider the idea that humans are part of nature as being one of the more significant ideas that Darwin alluded to. I believe that we need a shift in our understanding of the human/nature relationship; we must urgently adapt our behaviour so that we start to live *with* nature.

In 2009 I was lucky enough to be part of an adventure that, in some ways, took me closer to Darwin than I had been before. On board the Dutch ship *Stad Amsterdam*, we followed in the wake of Charles Darwin's voyage on HMS *Beagle* during the 1830s. This project, the brainchild of Hans Fels, was organised by Dutch television company VPRO. We travelled around the world to many of the same places that Darwin had visited some 180 years earlier: the Cape Verde Islands, Tierra del Fuego and, of course, the Galapagos Islands. We made 35 episodes for the television series 'The Future of the Species'. While filming in Brazil, where Darwin had raved in his typical understated way (see quotation above) about his experience in the tropical forest, two uncomfortable questions emerged for me. Are humans becoming more disconnected from nature? And if so, does it matter—either to nature or to humans?

A little delving into the literature revealed some answers. Humans apparently *are* becoming less and less connected to nature. Our children spend less time in nature than we did as children, and we in turn spent less time than our parents did. This is sad both for us and for nature. Of course, we humans need nature for our very survival; but we also need nature individually, because it makes us happier and healthier. In addition, research shows that people who spend time in nature are more willing to participate in the conservation of biodiversity.

So for me, one of the most important insights that Darwin brought us is that all living things are related; the oak tree, the orangutan, the squid in the sea and the orchid in the rainforest all share a single ancestor. And, of course, this includes us humans. We, too, are just one little twig on the tree of life, and we share our ancestry with all other living organisms on Earth. It seems logical that this knowledge would lead us to a greater feeling of connectedness with nature—and maybe even to a sense of responsibility towards our fellow creatures. But paradoxically, this is apparently not the case.

People often believe that to experience nature, you need to go to a distant rainforest. But nature is all around us—in our parks and gardens and local nature reserves. Indeed, Darwin intimately understood his local British biodiversity before joining the HMS *Beagle* crew. He had spent considerable time studying geology and the plants and animals around his home. This deep knowledge must have helped him realise that what he was seeing in the Brazilian forest or on the Galapagos Islands was different from what he had experienced back home—it must have helped him grasp the vastness of what we now call biodiversity.

For example, this spring I set up www.nightingale.berlin with two nightingale scientists in order to create a sound map of the Berlin nightingale populations. Here, citizen scientists with smartphones record their local nightingales within the city, and these sound files can then be added to the map of the city. This project gave us a chance not only to connect to our local seasonal nature—and to each other—but also to celebrate the arrival of spring with this extraordinary little bird. Understanding our local nature can help give us a sense of place and belonging.

After returning from his five-year voyage, Darwin never left Britain again. Indeed, after moving to the countryside with his wife Emma and their growing family, he rarely left his garden and the surrounding country. Much of the evidence he accrued for his theory of evolution was, in fact, found locally.

Darwin had a deep passion for nature; indeed, nature was his inspiration. It was because of this passion that he made his discoveries. His relationship with nature was as much an emotional one as an intellectual one: it brought him immense joy and was a constant source of knowledge and understanding. And maybe this is what I have learned more than anything from my great-great-grandfather: to keep my eyes and my mind open, to enjoy the wonders of nature and never cease to ask questions.

Sarah Darwin, PhD
Berlin September 2016

Acknowledgments

RESEARCH FOR THIS book has been facilitated greatly by the enormous amount of books, journals, letters, and other materials such as notebooks, diaries, and logbooks made available to the public through *Darwin Online* (www.darwin-online.org.uk) and the Darwin Correspondence Project (www.darwinproject.ac.uk).Both of these online resources offer a wealth of manuscripts, informative articles, and additional content; the search platforms on the sites are wonderfully easy to work with.

I am grateful for the inspiration and advice from my colleagues at the Natural History Museum of Denmark. They have been very helpful in commenting on various parts and at various stages of the manuscript, offering ideas, suggesting changes, and finding errors. I would especially like to thank Jens Astrup, Jørn Madsen, Thomas Pape, Minik Rosing, Ole Seberg, and Sven Stouge for comments on earlier versions of the book. They have caught many errors and have contributed toward making many points clearer and more precise.

I would also like to thank editors Ole Jørgensen and Axel Kielland at Gyldendal for comments and constructive advice on the manuscript. I am indebted to Catherine DeNardo and Errol Fuller, who have offered thoughtful advice and very valuable feedback on both content and composition of the book.

Graham Timmins translated the book from Danish to English and did an excellent job of not just translating the words but also identifying and catching the tone. He also took it upon himself to do a great deal of fact checking and clarification of the content, thereby improving the book significantly.

I am thankful for the careful reading and the suggestions for improvement that I have received from my copyeditor, Roberta Scholz. She did much more than find mistakes and errors (although there were certainly a lot of them); she also tweaked the language and identified confusing or misleading writing and suggested better alternatives. Like the translator, she improved the book greatly.

I would like to thank the Darwin Correspondence Project for permission to quote from Darwin's letter of February 13, 1882 to R.L. Tate, especially Rosemary Clarkson for being very helpful and for providing me with the correct quotation. For all the other letters quoted in the book as well as quotations from *Charles Darwin's Beagle Diary*, I am grateful for the permission granted by Cambridge University Press. For permission to quote passages from *The Autobiography of Charles Darwin*, I wish to thank Dr. Horace Barlow. The quotations from *Darwin's Notebook B, Darwin's Beagle Animal Notes*, and *Darwin's Notes on Shooting* are included in the book by permission of the Syndics of Cambridge University Library, for which I am obviously very thankful.

Likewise, I am grateful for the permission granted by the Trustees of the Natural History Museum, London, to quote from Darwin's ornithological notes edited by Nora Barlow and published in the *Bulletin of the British Museum (Natural History)*. Permission to quote from *T. rex and the Crater of Doom* by Walter Alvarez was granted by Princeton University Press.

I spent countless hours in the history library at the Natural History Museum of Denmark and wish to thank librarian Hanne Espersen for giving me access to the library and helping me find old volumes of Darwin's books and publications.

Very special thanks go to Dr. Sarah Darwin for writing the beautiful foreword for this book. I am deeply honored by that—and very grateful for the valuable comments and corrections that she offered as well.

Lastly, of course, I thank my family and friends for their support while I was researching and writing the book—and, not least, for bearing with me in my obsession with Darwin.

CHAPTER 1

A young man matures

CHARLES DARWIN NEVER forgot his father's words. As an old man, looking back at his life's achievements and scribbling down his memoirs, the words came back to him. "You care for nothing but shooting, dogs, and rat-catching, and you will be a disgrace to yourself and all your family"[1], his father had once yelled at him when he was a boy.

Rarely has a father been so spectacularly wrong about his son as Darwin's father was on this occasion; but in all fairness, it must be said that at the time it wasn't completely untrue. As a boy, Darwin really *had* been much more interested in hunting and shooting than schoolwork, and his performance in school was mediocre at best.

Born February 12, 1809, to a wealthy upper middle-class family in Shrewsbury in the English Midlands, he enjoyed a normal boyhood for a child of his time and class. His father was a successful doctor, and the family resided in a gloomy mansion known as "The Mount". But when he was just eight, tragedy struck the family. His mother died after a period of illness, leaving the father with six children—of whom Darwin was the second-youngest. In retrospect, Darwin didn't remember much about his mother, and her early death doesn't seem to have traumatised him. Perhaps his doting sisters compensated for the loss; they certainly stepped in and took over the maternal duties in the house.

In his early years, Darwin was schooled by his elder sisters and by private tutors. At age nine, he was sent, together with his older brother Erasmus, to the local public school to get a more formal education. This was not a success. Formal education consisted almost entirely of Latin and Greek verses and did not catch young Darwin's interest at all. His own verdict on the years he spent there was unambiguous: "The school as a means of education to me was simply a blank"[2], he recalled in his memoirs. The surrounding landscape and nature offered a range of more tempting activities for a young boy. He fished, collected minerals and birds' eggs, conducted chemical experiments in the garden shed with his older brother Erasmus, rode horses, and of course went shooting. The shooting became almost an obsession, and he eagerly counted the number and species of his victims. Though always very modest about his abilities and achievements, he conceded in his memoirs that he was indeed a very good shot[3].

In 1825, when he was 16, his father sent both him and Erasmus to Edinburgh to study medicine, but this plan did not work out. Dissecting corpses and operating on patients without anaesthetic did not appeal to the young Darwin, so after two years of half-hearted studying—and plenty of extra-curricular activities—he left Edinburgh without taking the sought-after degree.

Before leaving Edinburgh, Darwin had made the acquaintance of Robert Grant, a young zoologist who taught natural history at the university and took students along on field trips to the Scottish coast. This was an important meeting for Darwin: not only did he find Grant a talented and inspiring teacher, but Grant introduced him to some of the latest thinking from the Continent about what was then called the transmutation of species—what we now call evolution.

Natural theology

These ideas were revolutionary in the deeply religious society of the time, where science and religion were not at loggerheads with each other but went pretty much hand in hand. One of the most widely accepted conceptualisations of the development of life on Earth at the time had been penned in 1802 by theologian and philosopher William Paley. His *Natural Theology* argued that nature was designed by a creator. "[S]uppose I had found a watch on the ground", he pointed out, "the inference we think is inevitable, that the watch must have had a maker—that there must have existed, at some time and at some place or other, an artificer or artificers who ... designed its use. Every indication of contrivance, every manifestation of design which existed in the watch, exists in the works of nature"[4]. This is exactly the same argument of "intelligent design" used today by creationists arguing against Darwinism.

Later in his life, Darwin would reject this argument, but at this time he was convinced by it. "The logic of this book and, as I may add, of his 'Natural Theology', gave me as much delight as did Euclid.... I did not at that time trouble myself about Paley's premises; and taking these on trust, I was charmed and convinced by the long line of argumentation",[5] he wrote thoughtfully in his memoirs.

As far back as antiquity, ideas had been formulated about how the different animals and plants were related to each other. Aristotle's *Great Chain of Being* describes a hierarchy of all life forms, from the lowest and most primitive at the bottom to the most advanced at the top—man, of course, above the other animals but just below the angels and the Creator. At the bottom of the chain, beneath snails and snakes, were plants and, below them, rocks and minerals. This formulation included the idea that each animal and plant had its own allocated place in creation, and that this place was fixed for all time.

Digging up old bones from underground

Towards the end of the 18th century and at the beginning of the 19th, however, speculation about the development of animal and plant species—their mutability, in other words—was on the increase. Europe was in the grip of the Industrial Revolution, new roads and railways were being built, canals and mines were being dug, and everywhere strange skeletons of prehistoric animals were turning up. Maybe it was too soon to be talking about the possibility of new species arising, but it rapidly became quite clear that older species could die out—for it was obvious that many of the fossilised bones belonged to animals which no longer existed.

The French natural historian Georges Cuvier, who was made a baron in 1829 for his services to natural sciences, was the first to describe an extinct animal. Cuvier was a remarkable man in several ways. As director of the natural history museum in Paris, he rode out the stormy years of the revolution, the Napoleonic empire, and the restoration of the monarchy without losing either his head, his position, or his title. This was an amazing achievement in itself, but he also had enormous influence on the development of palaeontology. An eminent anatomist, he reportedly could reconstruct an entire animal from just a single bone or tooth.

Before Cuvier, what we now know as fossilised mammoth bones had previously been taken for elephant bones. The fact that most such finds had been made in Siberia was explained away by the assumption that when elephants had lived there, the climate must have been much hotter. Cuvier, having determined that no living elephant species had similar teeth to the remains from Siberia, proposed the name "mammoth" for the animal—which he promptly declared to be extinct. In another paper the same year, he described the extinct giant sloth *Megatherium*, a species which Darwin would later encounter in Patagonia. Cuvier subsequently identified two long-extinct reptiles, the marine lizard *Mosasaurus* and the bird-like *Pterodactylus*.

Cuvier's work involved breaking with the idea of a *Scala Natura*, an unbroken chain of species from the most humble to the most elevated, as the underlying principle of nature. Apparently, individual species could entirely disappear without creating any problems for the remaining species. His observations also raised another question: Why *had* certain species disappeared, anyway?

Cuvier decided that extinction must be due to catastrophic environmental changes, and his ideas came to form the basis of a new theory known as catastrophism. Since many remains of extinct animals were found in marine deposits, Cuvier thought it probable that violent natural events leading to sudden inundations of large areas of land had caused entire species to die out. He himself never linked this idea with the Biblical story of the Flood, but others were not slow to make the connection. This was especially the case amongst English speakers who had read the not entirely accurate translation of Cuvier's writings made by Robert Jameson. (Jameson even added his own notes to the original text, putting Cuvier's theory into what he thought was its correct Biblical context.) Darwin himself would fall under Jameson's influence as a student in his natural history classes at Edinburgh, if not in a positive way. "During my second year at Edinburgh, I attended Jameson's lectures on Geology and Zoology, but they were incredibly dull. The sole effect they produced on me was the determination never as long as I lived to read a book on Geology, or in any way to study the science",[6] wrote Darwin. A promise which, fortunately, he failed to keep!

Coming and going of species

At the same time as Cuvier in France was thinking about mammoths and other extinct species, an English land surveyor with no scientific training was making some important discoveries. William Smith was employed as supervisor of the digging of the Somerset Coal Canal, where he noticed different types of fossils in the layers of rock exposed during the excavations. Fossils typical of one layer, and thus of one geological period, could be entirely absent from the adjacent layers, which in turn featured a set of quite new and equally characteristic fossils. Smith saw that fossils had clearly been deposited in a sequence; what's more, he found the same sequences repeated at widely separated locations throughout England.

Back in the Paris basin, Cuvier made similar discoveries. The fossils in the lowest and therefore oldest layers disappeared and were replaced by others, which after another period of time also vanished from the record. This observation was not inconsistent with Cuvier's theory of catastrophism: it looked like life on Earth had repeatedly been wiped out and then re-created in new forms.

Cuvier was not the only man in France trying to fathom the comings and goings of species. He wasn't even the only one at the natural history museum in Paris. Two of his colleagues were working with the same questions but coming to different conclusions. The youngest of these was Étienne Geoffroy Saint-Hilaire, who was interested in homologous structures in nature—that is to say, forms which are fundamentally the same even though their appearances may well be different.

Saint-Hilaire ascertained, amongst other things, that vertebrate bones are homologous. When he examined the limbs of a man, an ape, a mole, or even a whale or a bird, he found that they were made up of the same types of bones, put together in the same way. If these animals had been individually created by God, it didn't make any sense that they should be designed according to the same pattern. That pointed rather to their being related to each other. This issue became a matter of some dispute between Saint-Hilaire and Cuvier. However, such heretical ideas were already widespread in scientific circles by that time and continued to inspire others, including Darwin, who would refer to Saint-Hilaire when he published *On the*

Origin of Species in 1859. Saint-Hilaire was one of the few he deemed as "tending on the mutability-side"[7] when he performed head counts to determine who among his fellow scientists and naturalists was in favour of his revolutionary ideas.

Lamarck

But in Paris, Cuvier had to contend with not only Saint-Hilaire but also the somewhat older Jean-Baptiste Lamarck, the first scientist to attempt to formulate a coherent theory of evolution. He, too, had proposed a set of mechanisms for how evolution worked. In 1809, the year Darwin was born, Lamarck published his *magnum opus*, the *Philosophie Zoologique*, in which he explained the forces he thought were at play. His ideas met with serious resistance (not least from Cuvier), but they also won widespread acceptance. However, when it became Darwin's turn to enter the arena, he dismissed Lamarck's ideas entirely. "Heaven forfend me from Lamarck nonsense"[8], he wrote to a friend when he first lifted the veil on his theory of evolution. Yet he readily admitted that his own conclusion—that life evolved continuously—was the same as Lamarck's. It was the driving force *behind* evolution that they didn't agree on. For Lamarck, this force consisted of two different forces.

The first he dubbed the "complexifying force"—meaning that species were always progressing towards states of greater complexity and refinement. New organisms—simple, microscopic forms—were continually appearing by means of "spontaneous generation" (out of thin air, in other words) and gradually developing into "higher", more advanced forms of life. In Lamarck's view, there was no extinction of species, just transformation into something else.

The second component of Lamarck's theory of evolution was the "adaptive force", by which organisms developed in relation to their environments. He described how waterfowl would gradually grow longer legs as they searched for food in deeper water, and how their feet would become webbed as they tried to avoid sinking into the mud encountered at greater depths. And he postulated that a giraffe, constantly stretching to reach the leaves higher up on trees, would gradually develop a longer neck. This much represented only what was widely accepted at the time. But Lamarck took an extra step, one he is still famous for today. He stated that not only would the giraffe get a longer neck, but so would its descendants: the trait would be *inherited* by its offspring. In the same way, lack of use an organ or body part would lead to its being lost in future generations. Here, he relied on his observations of certain mole rats, which live underground and have eyes so tiny that the animals are effectively blind.

Darwin called this "rubbish", but it was especially this latter part of Lamarck's theory, the inheritance of acquired traits, that many others thought plausible. When Lamarck spoke of species that were not 'immutable' but rather could change over time, and of species resembling each other because they were *related*—rather than because the Creator had gotten carried away with the idea of making a series of variations on the same theme—it made sense to those not bound by religious dogma.

Too much speculation, too few facts

Darwin had been introduced to Lamarck's ideas through Robert Grant, whom he had met in Edinburgh. Grant had studied in Europe, had spent time in Paris, and was deeply influenced by both Lamarck and Saint-Hilaire. Although Darwin was not actually enrolled in any of Grant's courses at the university, he became one of his keenest students. On many field trips with Grant around the Firth of Forth, Darwin received thorough training in observing and describing the marine organisms of that coastline—skills which would stand him in good stead years later on the voyage of the *Beagle*. But the young Darwin was not yet ready for revolutionary ideas. In old age, looking back on his time in Scotland, he remembered how Grant had sung the praises of Lamarck and his evolutionary theories. "I listened in silent astonishment, and as far as I can judge without any effect on my mind",[9] recalled Darwin.

Darwin was also exposed to ideas about evolution from a source much closer to hand. In the 1790s, his grandfather, Erasmus Darwin, published his book *Zoonomia*. This was probably the first book in England to unambiguously suggest that all warm-blooded animals might have arisen from a common origin, a "living filament". But his grandfather's book did not leave a strong impression on young Charles, either. Writing his memoirs, he recalled his grandfather's words and his views on a common origin; but he also stated that they hadn't had any effect on him. "Nevertheless it is probable that hearing rather early in life such views maintained and praised may have favoured my upholding them under a different form in my 'Origin of Species'",[10] he admitted.

However, his grandfather's work may have influenced Darwin in other ways. "At this time I admired greatly the 'Zoonomia'; but on reading it a second time after an interval of ten or fifteen years, I was much disappointed; the proportion of speculation being so large to the facts given", he continued. Perhaps it was at this point that Darwin decided not to make the same mistake.

CHAPTER 2

Keys to the future

FOLLOWING HIS SOJOURN in Edinburgh, Darwin spent the next years in Cambridge, where he would get on much better. Following his abandonment of the study of medicine, his father had suggested he take up the priesthood instead; after taking some time to consider, Darwin accepted this proposition.[1] This was not a decision motivated by any deep religious conviction; the livelihood of a country parson was simply a rather comfortable one, and one of the few considered suitable for a gentleman. Above all, it was quite acceptable for a man of the cloth to study natural history on the side, and it was becoming ever clearer and clearer that this was where his chief interests lay. Apart from the obligatory classes in Greek and Latin at Cambridge, Darwin now threw himself into the study of insects. A passionate beetle collector, he at first complained that he was "dying by inches, from not having any body to talk to about insects".[2] Luckily, he would soon get to know professor of botany John Henslow and geology professor Adam Sedgwick. Under the wings of these men, Darwin's interests expanded greatly, and he progressively acquired significant experience in new fields of natural history by means of extra-curricular lectures, field trips, and informal study groups. He was not so enthusiastic about the classics and theology curricula, however, and he had to work hard to pass the exams for his B.A. in the spring of 1831.

Although Darwin had graduated successfully, he hesitated to retire immediately to a life of rural domesticity. He wanted to travel and explore and was disappointed when an anticipated expedition to the Canary Islands fell through. But then he had an extraordinary stroke of luck. Henslow had been asked to recommend a naturalist to accompany a surveying and exploration voyage on board the brig *HMS Beagle*—and he proposed Darwin for the post. The voyage, planned to take two years charting the coastlines of South America, would later be extended to five years and include a circumnavigation of the globe. Although this was not explicitly stated, the main purpose of advertising the post was to secure a "gentleman travelling companion" for the 26-year-old captain, Robert FitzRoy. It was lonely at the top of the social hierarchy on board an early-19th-century sailing ship, and many did not cope well under these circumstances. FitzRoy's predecessor on the *Beagle* had shot himself off the coast of Patagonia; his uncle, also a sea captain, had cut his own throat.

FitzRoy, in other words, wanted someone to shield him from the worst of the loneliness of his position. The strict discipline on board ship made it impossible for a captain to be on familiar terms with any of his subordinates. However, with an independent naturalist in the next cabin, FitzRoy would have someone to chat with, to discuss scientific questions with, and to share a bottle of claret with. Darwin's role was to keep FitzRoy company and otherwise not get in the way.

Darwin was, of course, delighted with the opportunity. Here was a chance to explore the exotic landscapes of South America, where there would be all sorts of specimens of unrecorded flora and fauna to collect. However, his father—who would need to fund Darwin's expenses on the trip—was not at all impressed and wrote out a long list of objections. Amongst other points, he was concerned that such a journey would offer another excuse for Charles to change his course in life again and that it would be a complete waste of time. As we now know with the benefit of hindsight, he was as right about the former as he was wrong about the latter.

Darwin appealed to his uncle, Josiah Wedgwood, for backing. Luckily, Wedgwood immediately took up his nephew's cause and persuaded Robert Darwin that the voyage would do his son a world of good. So with his father's blessing and financial support, Darwin threw himself into preparations for departure. There were ropes, books, tools, and pistols to be bought, as well as a microscope and boxes of preserving jars for all the specimens Darwin planned to collect. The *Beagle* was a small ship, less than 100 feet in length, and with over 70 men on board there was not much room to spare. For the entire voyage, Darwin would share a cabin with two junior midshipmen, John Stokes and Philip King—who were only 19 and 14 years old, respectively, when the ship left England.

Posterity would link the voyage of the *Beagle* firmly with Darwin and his discoveries, but the actual purpose of the expedition was simply to survey the coastline of South America in order to provide accurate charts for the use of the Royal Navy and the British mercantile fleet.

When Darwin came aboard the *Beagle* for the first time and saw the cabin which would be his home for the next five years, he was quite shocked. In the tiny cabin, measuring only 10 by 11 feet, most of the space was taken up by the chart table in the middle, where John Stokes was to work on maps and measurements. Darwin would be allowed a corner of this table for pursuing his investigations into natural history, and he would have to sleep in a hammock strung up every evening over the top of the chart table and put away again in the morning.

Nevertheless, the young naturalist soon got used to the conditions on board the *Beagle*. Perhaps it was here that he developed the sense of order and fastidiousness which characterised him for the rest of his life. Darwin was appreciated by the rest of the crew for his friendly and accommodating manner. "I can confidently express my belief that during the five years in the *Beagle*, he was never known to be out of temper, or to say one unkind or hasty word *of* or *to* anyone",[3] recalled one of the crew. Another added: "I think he was the only man I ever knew against whom I never heard a word said; and as people when shut up in a ship for five years are apt to get cross with each other, that is saying a good deal".[4]

It was a different story with FitzRoy: the captain was not an easy man to live with. He had a violent temper and regularly lost his patience. "Is the coffee hot today?" was the crew members' coded enquiry as to the captain's mood of the day. If the answer was "Scalding!", it was best to keep out of his way. For a good while, though, Darwin was absolutely thrilled with FitzRoy, describing him as both polite and exceedingly accommodating; this feeling of regard was mutual. Later they had various differences, the worst of which arose within the context of a discussion about slavery, which Darwin abhorred and opposed and FitzRoy defended. This argument became so heated that FitzRoy threw Darwin out of his cabin. However, he soon regretted his temper and sent an officer with an apology, which Darwin happily accepted.

On board ship with *Principles of Geology*

Henslow had advised his protégé to procure a copy of the recently published first volume of *Principles of Geology* by Scottish geologist Charles Lyell. However, the professor—a believer in catastrophism, like all geologists of his day—warned Darwin "on no account to accept the views therein advocated"[5], referring to Lyell's contrary theory of gradual change over long aeons.

Darwin didn't need to buy a copy of *Principles of Geology*, because he had received one as a welcome-aboard gift from FitzRoy. This work would come to have enormous significance for Darwin and his thoughts on the development of life on Earth, for which reason FitzRoy would bitterly regret the gift later in life. For even as

Darwin doubted more and more the Bible's explanation of the story of creation and the origins of life, so FitzRoy became more and more fixed in his religious faith. When, many years later, Darwin published his book *On the Origin of Species*, his former travelling companion on the *Beagle* became one of his most fervent opponents.

Darwin devoured the *Principles* in the course of his first few weeks on board the *Beagle*—perhaps helped by the fact that sea sickness confined him to his hammock most days. The book's modest and understated subtitle, *An attempt to explain the former changes of the Earth's surface by reference to causes now in operation*, concealed the revolutionary idea that the forces which had shaped and changed the surface of the Earth had not stopped operating but, on the contrary, could still be observed today. In other words, observations made in the present were the key to understanding the past. This principle was one of the key ideas in Lyell's conception of geological processes and the history of the Earth and is often described as the *uniformity of process*.

Lyell's uniformitarianism also encompassed three further principles: the *uniformity of law*, stating that the laws of nature are the same throughout time and space; the *uniformity of rate* (later called *gradualism*), which assumed that changes in the Earth's geology occur slowly, regularly, and gradually rather than in sudden cataclysmic events; and the *uniformity of state*, or the hypothesis that the Earth has always looked and behaved pretty much like it does today. In other words: there is change, but it is not leading anywhere in particular—the Earth is in a dynamic but steady state.

Thus, according to Lyell, the Earth's appearance today is not the result of catastrophic upheavals, such as Cuvier had proposed as an explanation for the extinction of animal species, but rather the result of gradual action of geological forces *which can still be observed in the present*. The landscape we see is formed through erosion and sedimentation by wind and weather and by the constant chafing at the coastlines and river banks by seas and rivers. Finds of fossilised sea shells high up in the mountains are explained as a result of successive earthquakes gradually lifting the sea bed by thousands of metres.

Lyell also saw that the Earth must be many millions of years old in order to allow time for the gradual processes of geological formation which he described.

The idea that small modifications appearing slowly and gradually over a long period of time can create great changes, which Darwin got from Lyell's geology, would be the first piece of a jigsaw puzzle that would take him the next 25 years to complete. Lyell used this concept to explain the creation of the landscape, while Darwin would use it to explain the evolution of species.

Discoveries on land

The *Beagle*'s first port of call was Santiago in the Cape Verde islands off the West African coast. Darwin couldn't wait to get ashore, and he found the geology on Santiago very interesting, as he later described: "On entering the harbour, a perfectly horizontal white band, in the face of the sea cliff, may be seen running for some miles along the coast, and at the height of about forty-five feet above the water. Upon examination, this white stratum is found to consist of calcareous matter, with numerous shells embedded, such as now exist on the neighbouring coast".[6] With Lyell's words fresh in his mind, this was clear evidence that the land had risen in relation to the sea. His very first exploration, Darwin commented in his memoirs, showed him "the wonderful superiority of Lyell's manner of treating geology".[7]

When the *Beagle* arrived in Chile three years later, Darwin arranged an expedition on foot into the Cordillera Mountains, where at a height of 6,000 feet he found thick layers of marine fossils and a grove of petrified tree trunks embedded in alternating layers of submarine lava flow and volcanic sandstone.[8] The trees had been buried under water at some distant point in time, after which the land had slowly but surely risen thousands of metres.

The most dramatic evidence that the forces which had lifted the land were still operating also manifested itself in Chile, when Darwin experienced a strong earthquake in the coastal town of Valdivia. A few days later, there were "beds of putrid mussel-shells—still adhering to the rocks—ten feet above high-water mark".[9] The land had risen several metres! There could be no clearer demonstration of "the wonderful superiority of Lyell's manner". Darwin had found a mentor, and Lyell a new disciple. Of course, Lyell knew nothing of this yet, and neither of them knew how close their friendship would become in years to come.

FitzRoy shared Darwin's interest in natural sciences and joined him on many of his field trips. It seems that—at least at the beginning—he also shared Darwin's enthusiasm for Lyell's theories. He wrote later of having accompanied a friend (no doubt Darwin) "across vast plains composed of rolled stones bedded in diluvial detritus some hundred feet in depth" and admitted to having remarked that "this could never have been effected by a forty days' flood".[10] Later, FitzRoy's enthusiasm would cool somewhat. When he came to write up his journals of the voyage, he used an entire chapter to explain away his previous sentiments. He blamed these on being "led away by sceptical ideas, and knowing extremely little of the Bible".[11]

Both Darwin and Lyell read FitzRoy's laborious reinterpretations of his observations when they were published in 1839, four years after the *Beagle*'s return to England, and were clearly entertained. "You will be amused with FitzRoy's Deluge Chapter", wrote Darwin to his sister Caroline. "Lyell, who was here to-day, has just read it, and says it beats all the other nonsense he has ever read on the subject".[12]

Catastrophism in modern times

Lyell's ideas of slow and gradual changes in the Earth's surface gradually began to set the tone within scientific circles. Even though nobody disputed Cuvier's authority as an anatomist and palaeontologist, his idea of catastrophic upheavals affecting the entire Earth as the explanation for the extinction of species seemed less and less convincing. Gradualism and uniformitarianism seemed to have won out over catastrophism—until the 1980s, that is, when Cuvier received some unexpected redress 150 years after his death. About 66 million years ago, a mass extinction event killed off not only all the dinosaurs but three-quarters of all life on Earth at the time. In a 1980 paper, a team led by American physicist Luis Alvarez suggested that the Earth had been hit by a giant asteroid, big enough to cause global firestorms and to throw enough dust and debris into the atmosphere to darken the skies for a number of years.[13] The resulting "winter" would have had catastrophic consequences for all plants dependent on photosynthesis, all animals which grazed on these plants, and of course the predatory animals which fed on the herbivores.

The Alvarez team found several pieces of evidence for their hypothesis. First, there was a clear difference between the types of fossil species found in the layers before and after 66 million years B.P. (before the present). Next, there was something special about the layer of dark clay which marked that boundary in the geological record: it contained extraordinarily high levels of the element iridium. Iridium is extremely rare in the Earth's crust, but not in asteroids and meteorites. Alvarez proposed that a massive asteroid impact would release a lot of iridium into the atmosphere, which would later fall as fine dust over the entire planet and yield a high concentration of the element, such as we see today at what is now called the Cretaceous-Paleogene (K-Pg) boundary.

Alvarez and his geologist son, Walter, first investigated this boundary at Gubbio, Italy, where they found sediments containing levels of iridium 100 times higher than normal. However, a single observation was not enough, so they travelled next to Denmark, finding at Stevns Cliff a very clearly exposed example of the K-Pg boundary layer: a black line in the middle of an otherwise chalky white cliff. This black stripe is known locally as the "fish clay".

Walter Alvarez later wrote, "It was clear right away that something unpleasant had happened to the Danish sea bottom when that clay was deposited. The rest of the cliff was made of white chalk, a kind of soft limestone, which was full of fossils of all kinds, representing a healthy sea floor teeming with life. But the clay bed was black, smelled sulphurous, and had no fossils except for fish bones. During the time interval represented by this 'fish clay', the healthy sea bottom had turned into a lifeless, stagnant, oxygen-starved graveyard, where dead fish slowly rotted".[14] The fish clay at Stevns Cliff also turned out to contain massively raised levels of iridium, and samples of the K-Pg boundary layer from more than 100 other locations have since confirmed the Alvarez hypothesis of a gigantic asteroid strike.

Even more dramatic evidence was provided by the discovery of the Chicxulub impact crater on Mexico's Yucatán peninsula. Hidden under millions of years of sediments is a 180 km-wide crater thought to have been created by an extra-terrestrial object at least 10 km in diameter and dated to exactly 66 million years old.

Although the Alvarez hypothesis is now widely accepted by earth scientists, some dissenting voices favour an alternative explanation for the K-Pg mass extinction event: rather than an asteroid strike, a series of massive volcanic explosions. Either way, there is agreement that violent and catastrophic events affecting the entire Earth have at times wiped out most animal and plant life on the planet—more or less as Cuvier proposed.

Life itself affects the geology of the earth

That physical conditions on Earth have affected the development of life on our planet seems pretty obvious. However, what about the idea that living things in turn affect their surroundings—and even the geology of the planet?

In fact, this has been going on almost since the start of life on Earth. Well-known examples include chalk cliffs and limestone rocks composed of the compacted remains of tiny marine organisms and often containing larger fossils. The limestone escarpment at Wenlock Edge in Shropshire, just 13 miles from Darwin's childhood home in Shrewsbury, also features one of the finest examples anywhere of reef-building geology—revealing a legacy of coral-forming organisms which thrived in the Silurian period 425 million years ago. This was undoubtedly a fine place to find fossils, and Darwin most certainly visited it as a young man. In a letter to Charles Lyell written in 1841, he recalled: "I once saw close to Wenlock, something such as you describe, & made a rough drawing, I remember, of the masses of coral".[15]

Of course, all the coal, oil, and gas reserves in the world that have powered industrial society for the past 150 years are of purely organic origin, too. Even igneous rocks such as granite could not have formed without the presence of photosynthesising micro-organisms which produced the oxygen necessary to convert volcanic basalt into the feldspar, quartz, and mica minerals that compose granite[16]. Granite is lighter than basalt, so when tectonic plates collide, it floats on top, forming the great land masses which we—and much of life on Earth—inhabit today.

Thus, although Lyell contributed greatly to our understanding of Earth's geology and the development of life, he overlooked one crucial insight. Earth has not always looked like it does today; it has undergone massive changes over an unimaginable time scale of 4.5 billion years—and the most dramatic of those changes were initiated by living organisms themselves.

CHAPTER 3

Mysterious bones

As THE *BEAGLE* sailed around the South American coastline, taking soundings and measurements, Darwin seized every opportunity to get on shore. The land teemed with wonderful and unknown species, spectacular rock formations, and curiosities of all kinds—just waiting to be discovered, described, and understood. Darwin eagerly collected anything he could carry: flatworms, tiny crustaceans, beetles, butterflies, rock samples from different sedimentary layers, and as many fossils as he could find. The young naturalist worked very methodically, wrote out all his observations carefully in his log books, kept a diary, and wrote long letters home to his family and his mentor at Cambridge, John Henslow. Letters took a long time on their journey; moreover, one could send and receive post only when the ship was in harbour in a major town. Henslow was a knowledgeable and passionate natural historian, and no doubt Darwin felt a special obligation to keep him updated: after all, it was Henslow who had found him the position on the *Beagle*.

Darwin also received long letters from home. With such a large family, there was always some news. His sisters took special pains to keep him informed about anyone in their circles who had become engaged or had married (perhaps to tell him which eligible young ladies were therefore no longer available). Now it was his cousin, Frank Wedgwood, who was to marry a Miss Moseley; then it was the other cousin, William Fox, who was engaged to a Miss Fletcher. There was also a happy family event to report: his eldest sister, Marianne, had given birth to a boy who was to be christened Charles after his uncle.

Not all the letters brought happy tidings for Charles, however. His sister, Catherine, gently broke the news that a certain Fanny Owen had become engaged and would be a married woman by the time Darwin came home again[1]. Fanny had been more than a close friend, and a deeply shaken Darwin wrote back: "I find that my thoughts & feelings & sentences are in such a maze, that between crying & laughing I wish you all good night".[2] Another sister, Caroline, began one of her chatty letters by imagining how nice it would be when Charles was safely home again in England: "I am very much pleased to find the quiet Parsonage has still such charms in your eyes. It is so delightful to look forward & fancy you settled there—and in spite of this marrying year I am sure you will find some nice little wife left for you".[3]

Crucial discoveries

But Darwin was thinking less and less of a future life as a country parson. Caught up in the excitement of finding it so easy to interpret the geological strata at Santiago on the Cape Verde Islands, he was hatching an idea in his head. He would write a book on geology, a major work which would make his name as a man of science. He even tested the waters with his family, no doubt with an eye mainly towards his authoritarian father, by suggesting rhetorically: "And it appears to me, the doing what little one can to encrease [*sic*] the general stock of knowledge is as respectable an object of life, as one can in any likelihood pursue".[4]

Darwin was painfully aware that if he wanted to be accepted as a scientist, he needed to be the first to discover something. So it worried him greatly when he learnt that the French government had already sent a scientist to collect specimens in South America just before he got there himself. "I must have one more growl, by ill luck the French government has sent one of its Collectors to the Rio Negro—where he has been working for the last six month, & is now gone round the Horn.—So that I am very selfishly afraid he will get the cream of all the good things, before me", he complained in a letter to Henslow.[5] Still, in September 1832, luck was definitely on Darwin's side. Sailing along the coast of Patagonia, the *Beagle* came to Bahía Blanca. Darwin and FitzRoy went exploring along the shoreline in a small boat as far as the rocky outcrop of Punta Alta, where they found some low mudstone cliffs which turned out to contain huge numbers of extraordinary fossils.

The cliffs were only about ten feet high, and the reddish clay was so full of bones that some of them were poking out of the cliff face. Darwin and a boy set to work with pickaxes, and on the second day he found a cranium so big that it took three hours to dig it out. It was dark by the time they got back to the ship and added it to the pile of bones from the previous day's excavations, lying on the deck. At first Darwin thought the skull must be from some kind of rhinoceros,[6] but he soon realised that he had actually found a *Megatherium*, an extinct giant ground sloth the size of an elephant. (Its smaller cousins are still found in South America today.) "This is particularly interesting", commented Darwin, "as the only specimens in Europe are in the King's collection at Madrid, where for all purposes of science they are nearly as much hidden as if in their primaeval rock".[7]

The skeleton kept in Madrid had been excavated in 1789 in what is now Argentina. The bones were shipped to Madrid and mounted into a nearly complete skeleton by Juan Bautista Bru at the Royal Cabinet of Natural History. In 1796, drawings of the skeleton came into the hands of the great French anatomist Georges Cuvier, who published the first description of the animal. He named it *Megatherium americanum* and identified it as a relative of the contemporary tree-dwelling sloths, though the size of a smallish Indian elephant. Concluding it impossible that an animal of that size could still be living undetected in South America, he declared it extinct.

A month later, and 60 miles along the coast from Punta Alta, Darwin came upon another rich source of fossils at Monte Hermoso. It dawned on him that his growing collection of bones on the deck of the *Beagle* could, if he handled the situation well, be his admission ticket to scientific circles back in England.

He hastily had wooden crates made up to ship them back to England, writing modestly to his former professor John Henslow at Cambridge: "If it interests you sufficiently to unpack them, I shall be very curious to hear something about them."[8]

It certainly did interest Henslow, and he not only unpacked the fossils with great interest but also arranged for them to be presented at the annual meeting of the British Association for the Advancement of Science, where Darwin's description of the finds was also read out.[9] Little guessing how successful his efforts would ultimately be, Henslow did everything he could to promote his protégé. He even cobbled together a scientific paper out of Darwin's letters and notes and presented it in 1835 to the world of scholarship at the Cambridge Philosophical Society. Another one, for the Geological Society, followed in 1836.

Thus when Darwin eventually arrived home from the nearly five-year voyage of the *Beagle* in October 1836, his scientific observations and accounts—and not least the sensational finds from Patagonia—had indeed established his name in the most respected scientific circles. The great man Lyell himself had heard of Darwin and was looking forward to meeting him. Reading Darwin's descriptions, he recognised that the younger man had not merely *read* his book, he had *understood* it. Adam Sedgwick, like Henslow a former tutor from Darwin's Cambridge days, had also heard of his discoveries and had already commented to a common acquaintance: "He is doing admirably in S. America, & has already sent home a Collection above all praise.—It was the best thing in the world for him that he went out on the Voyage of Discovery—There was some risk of his turning out an idle man: but his character will now be fixed, & if God spare his life, he will have a great name among the Naturalists of Europe."[10]

Describing the finds

On Darwin's return to England, invitations flooded in from all quarters of the scientific community. One of the first was from Charles Lyell, who invited Darwin to his house in October 1836, only a few weeks after he got back. Lyell also introduced Darwin to Richard Owen, a young man who was very keen to meet him. Now 32, Owen was only five years older than Darwin, though certainly not so well travelled. He had started in the same way, with medical training at Edinburgh; like Darwin, he had changed course—in his case, to the study of anatomy and bones and thence to fossils, about which he was already something of an expert.

Owen was employed at The Royal College of Surgeons, which had its own museum, so he had already seen Darwin's *Megatherium* cranium. (It had been brought there from Punta Alta.)

The two young men agreed that Owen would examine and describe all the remaining fossil bones Darwin had shipped back from Patagonia. Not only did Darwin plan to write the traditional Victorian travel memoir describing his fantastic experiences—the book that would become *The Voyage of the Beagle*—he had a much grander scheme in mind. He would enlist the foremost experts in the country, of which Owen was just the first, to work on his collections from the journey and describe their findings. Not himself an expert in any of the fields but eager to make his mark within the scientific establishment, Darwin appointed himself editor and superintendent of the resultant series of learned volumes, which would emerge over the next five years.

Owen was the ideal man to take care of Darwin's fossils. He was a gifted anatomist with a comprehensive knowledge of many different animal groups, including both living and extinct species. He was also ambitious and unafraid of any obstacles which might stand in the way of an insight or a new scientific lead. With access to the cadavers of any animals that died in the care of the London Zoo, he had already dissected a gorilla, an elephant, and a rhinoceros—the last in the hallway of his home. His long-suffering wife was said to tolerate Owen's habit of bringing his work home, so long as he masked the stench of rotting cadavers with plenty of cigar smoke![11]

Owen set to work, piecing together the pile of bones from the *Beagle*. As it turned out, they represented many different species, including some quite unknown to science. Eventually the jigsaw puzzle was finished, revealing the more or less complete skeletons of no fewer than seven large prehistoric animals.

Darwin already knew he had bones from *Megatherium*, but three other extinct giant sloths were also represented. There was the carapace of a glyptodon, a kind of giant armadillo that had previously been described, and two other species which Owen struggled to place. He named one of them *Toxodon platensis*. Darwin had brought back several different pieces of the animal's cranium from Punta Alta but had also bought a much finer specimen (for the price of 18 pence) a few months later in Uruguay. The skull had been used for target practice by some boys who had thrown stones at it and knocked one of its teeth out. Fortunately, Darwin later found a tooth that matched the empty socket perfectly.[12] This skull was a puzzle for Owen. The animal was obviously enormous—at least as big as a hippopotamus—but the large, curved teeth persuaded him that it must in fact be a giant rodent.[13]

The second strange animal Owen had to put a name to lacked a skull altogether, but he did have a number of other bones—including vertebrae, a scapula, a femur, a tibia, and a tarsus. It was enough to determine it was a new species and as big as a camel, with long legs and a sturdy frame; in fact, Owen decided it was some kind of camelid and named it accordingly *Macrauchenia patachonica,* meaning "giant llama from Patagonia."[14]

Amongst all the *Megatherium* bones, Darwin had also found a horse's tooth.[15] This was quite a puzzle—after all, it was well known that the horse had been introduced to the Americas by European colonists only in the 16th century. Darwin thought the tooth couldn't possibly be the same age as the fossil bones. Owen, however, disagreed: the horse's tooth was contemporary with the large extinct animals and was evidence that horses had lived on the South American continent long before Europeans arrived. "This ... is not one of the least interesting fruits of Mr. Darwin's palæontological discoveries", wrote Owen with typical British understatement.[16] We now know for certain that Owen was right and that horses were widespread in the Americas until the end of the last ice age, when they suddenly died out.

Until the 20th century, there was no way of dating fossils directly or accurately, but Darwin and Owen did have a few clues to follow. In between the large bones, Darwin had found fossilised mussel shells, most of which were clearly of the same species as the ones still living in the waters around Punta Alta and Monte Hermoso. With this in mind, and seeing that the land masses in this area had risen only a tiny amount since the sediments were laid down, Darwin concluded that the bones were from a very recent epoch.[17] In other words, these prehistoric animals likely had lived contemporaneously with most of the South American animals alive in Darwin's day. Even though this may not sound like a very startling discovery, it was in fact a conclusion in complete opposition to accepted models of species extinction of that time. The Biblical idea of a world-wide flood taking everything with could not account for why most of an area's fauna—such as marine bivalves—carried on as before while certain others were wiped out.

Connection between extinct and living species

What began as a friendship between Owen and Darwin turned, over time, into bitter hostility. Few scientists would be so aggressive as Owen in the heated debate that followed publication of *On the Origin of Species* in 1859. So it is ironic that the finds of fossil remains of Patagonia's extinct fauna not only opened the doors for Darwin's entry into the inner circles of the English scientific establishment, but also opened Darwin's eyes to the evolution of species. What's more, this happened as a result of Owen's own work on *Toxodon*, which he compared with another large rodent, the capybara, a still-living South American species. The young anatomist noted: "It is highly interesting to find that the continent to which this existing aberrant form of Rodent is peculiar, should be found to contain the remains of an extinct genus on a gigantic scale."[18] Similarly, he wrote of the extinct *Macrauchenia* that it was "in a remarkable degree a transitional form, and manifests characters which connect it both with the Tapir and the Llama".[19] Perhaps it was just these remarks which set Darwin thinking about the relationship between extinct and living species— and the possibility of there being a connection between them.

The fossils from Punta Alta and Monte Hermoso were in every way of great significance for Darwin. In his books, he returned several times to the theme of how it had struck him that there was a connection between the species currently inhabiting an area and the fossil species found in the same region. Indeed, the very first lines of *On the Origin of Species* touch on just this relationship: "When on board H.M.S. *Beagle*, as naturalist, I was much struck with certain facts in the distribution of the inhabitants of South America, and in the geological relations of the present to the past inhabitants of that continent. These facts seemed to me to throw some light on the origin of species—that mystery of mysteries, as it has been called by one of our greatest philosophers.[20]

The final irony of this story is that Owen was wrong about the genealogy of both *Toxodon* and *Macrauchenia*. Since his day, more fossil material and closer investigations have revealed that neither species has any living relatives, whether in South America or elsewhere. *Toxodon* is not a rodent after all, but belongs instead to an order of hoofed mammals called *Notungulata*, which has no surviving relatives today. Nor does *Macrauchenia* have anything to do with llamas, camels, or tapirs: it belongs to another order of extinct hoofed animals with no living members, the *Litopterna*. Darwin had thus based his speculations about the relationship between living and extinct animals partly on incorrect assumptions. There is, however, no doubt that the extinct giant ground sloths are related to the living tree sloths, or that glyptodonts are related to armadillos.

Extinction was not a local phenomenon

In early 1832, as the *Beagle* lay at anchor off Rio de Janeiro, Danish zoologist and soon-to-be palaeontologist Peter Wilhelm Lund passed through the same city on his way to settle in eastern Brazil. Another former medical student who had been gripped by the natural history bug, P.W. Lund at first studied and collected everything he came across, from ants to snails to birds. But in 1835, he underwent an almost Pauline revelation which led him to switch to the speciality for which he would become famous. In the karst landscape around Lagoa Santa, Lund discovered a series of spectacular caves containing the fossilised bones of an entire Ice Age megafauna. He dedicated the next eight years to excavating no less than 20,000 of these and shipping them back to Copenhagen. As well as mastodons and other species Darwin never encountered, Lund's haul of extinct prehistoric animals included several species of giant sloths and glyptodons identical to the ones Darwin was finding in Argentina. Darwin would become aware of this when he read Lund's descriptions in translation after his return to England. It was clear that Darwin's *Megatherium* and *Glyptodon* could not be relics of a population wiped out by a local catastrophe; they were representatives of a continent-wide fauna. Some other cause must have driven them to extinction.

Megafauna

Just as it's hard to understand the scale of numbers when politicians talk about millions and billions of pounds or dollars—when our own household budgets are counted in mere thousands of pounds or dollars—it can be hard to grasp similar numbers on the geological scale and to fit the events and phenomena described into their proper places. Sometimes people get the vague impression that all large prehistoric animals were a kind of dinosaur and that they lived at about the same time. However, giant sloths and glyptodons were certainly no dinosaurs, and they lived only a split second ago in geological terms: namely, up until only 10,000 or 15,000 years ago. In other words, they were fully contemporaneous with modern human beings—unlike dinosaurs, the last of which vanished 65 million years ago.

The fauna of South America at the end of the last ice age included many species known today, but also a large number which are now extinct. In addition to several species of glyptodonts and giant sloths, there were also the sabre-toothed tiger, a small elephant known as *Stegomastodon*, and—of course—our friends *Toxodon* and *Macrauchenia*. All these large mammals belong to what we now call the megafauna: large or very large animals formerly found not just in South America but all over the world. During the same very recent period when giant sloths and glyptodons lived in South America, mammoths, Irish elk, woolly rhinoceros, cave bears, and steppe bison lived in Europe. In Australia, there were giant kangaroos and giant wombats. North America was home to mammoths and mastodons as well as to American lions and sable-toothed tigers. Except in Africa, where megafauna still run around on the savannah, there are only insignificant remnants of this fauna surviving today. The largest animal in North America now is the bison, and in Europe the European elk.

In most parts of the world, this megafauna had existed at the same time as human beings, and it was P.W. Lund who first confirmed this. In 1843, when excavating the lowest levels of one of the Lagoa Santa caves, he was intrigued to find 30 human skulls and other bones mixed with the prehistoric animal bones. The inference was clear: human beings had populated South America long before Europeans arrived, and they had co-existed with the extinct megafauna. Clearly, this discovery also contradicted Cuvier's catastrophe theory, although Lund never commented on this himself.

Long before it became a hot topic, Lund's discovery touched on a discussion which is still ongoing. Was the demise of the megafauna the fault of humans, or was it due to other factors such as climate change? Gavin Prideaux of Flinders University in Australia has no doubts: his research in Australia shows that the megafauna populations there were relatively stable for over 500,000 years. Periods of climate change did lead to fluctuations in populations, but then they stabilised again rather than going extinct. Prideaux compared his results with corresponding data from North America and commented: "These records show that mammal faunas on both continents were well adapted to Quaternary climatic variations prior to the arrival of humans".[21] That means the finger points to man as the essential reason for the disappearance of the megafauna, especially since time and again extinction occurred within a few thousand—or even a few hundred—years of human colonisation of a region. This may have been a direct result of hunting, or due to habitat changes as a result of bush and forest fires set by men, or a combination. The case is not yet closed, however: there is still heated debate in scientific circles as to whether the activities of prehistoric man were the main agent of extinction or only a contributory factor.

The fossil sites today

Human influence on the natural environment has not ceased, as is well known. The low cliffs of Punta Alta, where Darwin excavated his fossil treasures, have been levelled and buried under the car parks and lawns surrounding the Puerto Belgrano naval base. At Monte Hermoso, it's impossible to locate the exact place where Darwin excavated, because continual erosion is constantly uncovering new layers; however, large numbers of fossils can still be found in the area, and Argentinian palaeontologists are still at work there. Recently, an entire series of fossilised footprints of prehistoric animals—including *Megatherium*—was uncovered on the beach below the cliffs. Amongst the massive prints of giant sloths, one can see the much smaller tracks of *Macrauchenia* and glyptodons. This was a busy place in prehistoric times, and it still is: all summer long, the 10,000-year-old tracks of extinct megafauna are obliterated by more modern tracks as four-wheel-drive vehicles roar up and down the beach, heedless of its history.

CHAPTER 4

There's something about islands

SEVERAL TIMES IN the course of the *Beagle*'s long voyage, Darwin ran into a problem which many years later would lead him to another important piece in his understanding of how species evolve. Why are certain species found in one geographic area, while similar but slightly different species inhabit another, often adjacent, region? Fortunately for Darwin, FitzRoy was a thorough man who took his mission of surveying the South American coastline very seriously. This gave Darwin plentiful opportunities to spend long periods on land exploring whichever local features caught his interest. Often he would hire—or even buy—a horse and go on longer trips, riding with the Argentinian gauchos over the vast pampas.

For those who tend to think of Darwin as a sober old man with a long, white beard, here is an opportunity to conjure up a different image. The young Charles Darwin was more of a 19th-century Indiana Jones: tall, slim, athletic, always ready to climb a mountain or trek on horseback day after day. He happily hunted and shot his own game for dinner, cooked it on a campfire, and then slept out under the stars. He wrote home with satisfaction: "I am become quite a Gaucho, drink my Mattee & smoke my cigar, & then lie down & sleep as comfortably with the Heavens for a Canopy as in a feather bed".[1] Darwin may not actually have acquired all the skills of a gaucho, but he certainly wasn't afraid to have a go. A trial of the cattle-herders' bolas resulted in his immobilising his own horse. "The Gauchos roared with laughter", Darwin confessed; "they cried they had seen every sort of animal caught, but had never before seen a man caught by himself".[2]

It was the gauchos who drew Darwin's attention to a rare kind of bird, one very similar to the flightless rheas which they often hunted and ate. They called it the "Avestruz petise" and described it as smaller and darker than the normal rhea and with feathers all the way down its legs. Darwin searched for this bird for a long time, to no avail. Eventually he found it: on Christmas Eve, on board the *Beagle*—in a stew pot. He had in fact heard that one of the crew had shot a bird, and he had even seen the carcase—without paying attention. Only after the meal was well under way did it occur to him that the meat on his plate could be from that very "Avestruz petise" he was so keen to acquire a specimen of. Darwin managed to salvage the head, neck, legs, skin, and feathers and send them off to Henslow.[3]

The gauchos were correct: this was a different species of rhea, and the renowned ornithologist John Gould, whom Darwin enlisted to examine all his bird specimens from the voyage, initially named it: *Rhea darwinii*. However, the bird had already been given the Latin name by which it is known today, *Rhea pennata*. Darwin's anxiety that emissaries of the Paris Museum would get all the exciting specimens before he did was not unfounded: Alcide D'Orbigny had already caught and named a specimen, as was his right. However, the two naturalists later developed great mutual respect, and it was D'Orbigny who gave the rhea the common name it still bears in English—Darwin's rhea—in honour of his rival.

Darwin's rhea is most at home to the south of the range of its larger cousin, the American rhea. Darwin just happened to be in the overlap zone between the two ranges when he heard about the bird. But the rheas were only a foretaste of the problems Darwin would face in separating similar species from one another. The next time this would be a serious issue was in 1835, when the Beagle, after three and half years of sailing up and down the coast of South America, headed out into the Pacific Ocean and came to the Galápagos Islands.

The Galápagos

Darwin's encounter with the unique flora and fauna of the Galápagos is probably the event which in most minds today is linked with the development of his theory of evolution. However, sad to say, Darwin didn't simply have an epiphany as he sprang ashore on Chatham Island on September 18, 1835. He had looked forward eagerly to getting there, but mostly because it meant that the journey homewards had finally begun. In his last letter home to England from South America, he made no secret of the fact that the voyage was dragging on far too long for him; when in Lima he saw a vessel which was heading for England, he was almost tempted to jump ship.[4]

However, there was another reason Darwin was happy to visit the Galápagos: he knew their origin was volcanic, and he therefore expected the geology to be interesting. "I look forward to the Galápagos, with more interest than any other part of the voyage", he wrote home from Lima. "They abound with active Volcanoes & I should hope contain Tertiary strata".[5] He didn't expect to find much of botanical interest but thought that the animal life would definitely be worth investigating. In this respect, he was of course correct, but that realisation would dawn only slowly. Chatham Island was very different from the green and leafy forests of South America: "Nothing could be less inviting than the first appearance. A broken field of black basaltic lava is everywhere covered by a stunted brushwood, which shows little signs of life".[6]

Darwin plodded around in the heat, dutifully collecting both plants and animals, but apparently without much enthusiasm. He was, however, fascinated by the tameness of the wildlife—including a hawk, which he could push around with the butt of his gun. Other animals could simply be picked up with the bare hands, as one poor marine iguana experienced when Darwin visited another of the islands: "One day I carried one to a deep pool left by the retiring tide, and threw it in several times as far as I was able. It invariably returned in a direct line to the spot where I stood".[7]

Darwin collected a good number of the islands' different bird species, but there was nothing much which really grabbed his attention. The famous Galápagos finches, which are so strongly linked by posterity with his name and his theory of evolution, hardly got a mention in his diaries. On October 1, the crew went ashore on Albemarle Island to find drinking water, with little success: "To our disappointment the little pits in the Sandstone contained scarcely a Gallon & that not good", wrote Darwin later in his journal. "It was however sufficient to draw together all the little birds in the country. Doves & Finches swarmed round its margin".[8] That was all he said about finches at the time.

The *Beagle* stayed in the Galápagos archipelago for a good month before setting course for Tahiti. Down in his cabin, Darwin began to examine carefully the plants and animals he had collected on the various islands; he discovered that the birds were more interesting than he had first thought. It wasn't the finches that caught his attention, but rather some mockingbirds—a group he knew from South America. He had collected mockingbirds from four different islands, and now it struck him that he had four different types, even though they all lived under very similar conditions.

Suddenly he remembered that he had come across this phenomenon once before during the *Beagle*'s long voyage. On the Falkland
Islands, where the conscientious FitzRoy naturally carried out soundings as well, he had encountered the indigenous Falkland Islands
wolf. Like other animals on these only recently inhabited islands, the
fox-like wolves were exceptionally curious and unafraid, so much so
that the gauchos could kill them merely by luring them with a piece
of meat in one hand and a knife in the other. Darwin feared, with
justification, that such naïve trust would soon lead the wolves to share
the fate of the extinct dodo. Sadly, this prediction came true when the
last wolf died in 1876.[9] The *Beagle* had nevertheless brought home
four specimens, and Darwin recorded that the animal was unique to
the Falklands and was entirely unrelated to any canid found on the
mainland. Moreover, he recorded a report that the West Falkland
and East Falkland Islands each had their own type of wolf: the East
Falkland variety was said to be both bigger and darker-coloured.[10]

Darwin's first thoughts about evolution?

The English vice-governor of the Galápagos, Nicholas Lawson, had
told the crew of the *Beagle* that he could tell which island a giant
tortoise came from just by looking at its shell.[11] And now these mockingbirds! Darwin ruminated over the mockingbirds, cautiously making the first entry in his notebooks—revealing perhaps that he was
already on the track of something. "I have specimens from four of the
larger islands; the specimens from Chatham and Albemarle Islands
appear to be the same, but the other two are different. In each island
each kind is exclusively found; habits of all are indistinguishable". In
typical style, he continued by listing all the examples of variation he
already knew of, slowly amassing his evidence: "When I recollect the
fact, that from the form of the body, shape of scales & general size, the

Spaniards can at once pronounce from which island any tortoise may have been brought;—when I see these Islands in sight of each other and possessed of but a scanty stock of animals, tenanted by these birds but slightly differing in structure & filling the same place in Nature, I must suspect they are only varieties. The only fact of a similar kind of which I am aware is the constant asserted difference between the wolf-like Fox of East & West Falkland Islands". Suggesting where to look for further evidence, he finally raises the spectre of species not necessarily being something fixed, preordained and eternal: "If there is the slightest foundation for these remarks, the Zoology of Archipelagoes will be well worth examining; for such facts would undermine the stability of species".[12]

This last sentence has been much quoted and discussed in books on Darwin. Was it here that he first pondered whether species could evolve? One of the contemporary explanations for the presence of different flora and fauna in different areas was that they belonged to different "centres of creation". An area such as an island group was supposed to represent a centre of creation in which a certain degree of development or deviation from the norm could take place. Lyell was one of the spokespersons for this idea, and Darwin was of course very familiar with it. In *Principles of Geology*, Lyell had suggested that, if new volcanic islands should arise in proximity to the island of St. Helena, then plants would spread to them and gradually diverge from their original form.[13]

It has never been determined whether Darwin intended to argue with the established explanations when he wrote this sentence about facts that would undermine the stability of species. It is, however, clear that his tussling with what we would today call the biogeographical question did play a large role in the development of what would later become his coherent theory of the origin of species. He had seen with his own eyes that the species found on the islands were often different from those on the nearest piece of mainland, and he had deduced that the distribution of animals (and for that matter, of plants) in different geographical areas was not accidental but instead dependent on a long series of different factors. In a notebook a few years later, he sketched the idea that this kind of separation and variation in animals could lead to change—clearly with the rheas of Argentina in mind. "I look at two ostriches as strong argument of possibility of such change, as we see them in space, so might they in time".[14]

Island flora and fauna

Darwin had already noticed that the Galápagos fauna was very different from the fauna he knew from the mainland. Particularly conspicuous was the absence of mammals, a feature which he also noticed on other islands during the course of the voyage. It was also obvious that the iguanas and tortoises were unique to the Galápagos. Only later would he realise that this was equally true of most of the birds and plants as well.

What Darwin observed on the Galápagos, in New Zealand, and on Tahiti turned out to be a feature of islands in general. Many island species are endemic, meaning they are not found anywhere else in the world. The percentage of endemic species on islands is greater than in areas of comparable size on the mainland; the larger an island or island group is, and the further away it is from the mainland, the greater the percentage. On Hawaii, which is about as far as it is possible to be from anywhere else, 90 percent of all species found are endemic. Also typical is that many mammals inhabiting a nearby mainland are absent from islands. The mammals most commonly found on islands are bats, since they can fly there. Other mammal groups, such as predatory carnivores, are often entirely missing. This also explains why birds and other larger animals on islands tend to be very trusting of man, appearing to be tame.

Islands today still interest natural historians and biologists as much as they did in Darwin's time. Modern studies of the Galápagos and other islands show that animal and plant life evolves faster on islands than on the mainland; the evolution rate is higher, one could say.[15] One contributing factor is that islands typically host a more restricted range of species. With less competition, a species can exploit an opening which would not exist in areas where every ecological niche is already covered by a suitably adapted species.

There are other, more surprising, consequences of evolution on islands. For example, many island species are either much bigger or much smaller than their mainland cousins. According to the so-called island rule, species tend to evolve in size in accordance with the resources available in their environment. A large mammal finding itself in the restricted pastures of an island will get smaller over time, while a small one that is preyed upon on the mainland may become bigger in the absence of predators. From remains found in Sicily, we know of dwarf elephants the size of a deer[16]; Crete, Cyprus, Malta, and Sicily were all home to pygmy hippopotamuses in prehistoric times.[17] On the other hand, giant flightless birds once thrived on some islands. Madagascar was host to the biggest: the three-metre-tall elephant bird, which weighed as much as a medium-sized bull and may have survived into the 18th century. New Zealand, meanwhile, had plenty of moas—similar creatures hardly bothered by predators until the arrival of man in the early 14th century. Prior to their extinction in the mid-15th century, there were at least 10 species of moa on New Zealand's two islands; the largest was even taller than the elephant bird, though not as heavy.

The elephant bird, the moas, the dodo from Mauritius, and countless other birds and animals not only share their large size but also the fact that they have gone extinct, a common occurrence with island species. The lack of any inborn fear of man, in addition to the lack of an adapted ability to cope with introduced species such as rats, pigs, goats, dogs, and cats, was catastrophic for endemic island species and continues to be a major problem in places where they persist to this day. From several hundred to a few thousand unique island species have been wiped out in the past few hundred years. In most cases, there is a clear connection between the islands' colonisation by man and the rapid disappearance of endemic species.

In terms of evolutionary biology, islands are not simply pieces of land encircled by sea. Any geographical area in which plants and animals are effectively isolated from their surroundings can function just like an island. Large lakes can also host their own endemic fauna, among them Lakes Tanganyika, Malawi, and Victoria in East Africa. Here, thousands of different species of cichlids have evolved in a relatively short time. Cichlids are freshwater fish found all over the world, but nowhere are there so many species as in the large East African lakes. In Lake Victoria alone, hundreds of different cichlid species have been counted, with quite different lifestyles: some specialised to graze on algae, some to crunch up freshwater snails, some to prey on other fish, some even to live by nibbling the scales of other fish. However, just as on true islands, the ecosystem of a lake is vulnerable. After the introduction of the Nile perch to Lake Victoria, literally hundreds of cichlid species were either eradicated or brought to the edge of extinction.

High mountains can also function as biological islands. Here, much of the flora and fauna can develop in isolation from surrounding areas, often leading to greater species diversity. One such biological hotspot, and one of the richest in numbers of species, is the Eastern Arc mountain chain in Tanzania. Here, in an area of 2,000 square kilometres, over 1,500 endemic plant species and 121 endemic vertebrate species may be found—more per square kilometre than almost anywhere else on Earth.[18] New species are being described all the time; as recently as 2008, something as unusual as a new *mammal* was found. The grey-faced sengi belongs to the order of mammals previously known as elephant shrews, but this one is much bigger than any other sengi—almost the size of a small dog, in fact. It had remained undescribed despite its size because it lives in dense forest high in the mountains; only when visiting scientists used a camera trap was it detected. New species of reptiles, amphibians, birds, and plants are everyday discoveries for the lucky biologists who work in this exciting area.

Alfred Wallace

As Darwin was uncovering fossils at Punta Alta, he at first thought that the massive cranium he would drag back to the *Beagle* came from some sort of rhinoceros. Later, learning that it was, in fact, a giant sloth and thus related to contemporary South American sloths, he began to see some patterns in species distribution among continents. At this large scale, certain animal groups (such as the Edentata, the order to which both sloths and armadillos belong) clearly had always belonged to South America and never existed anywhere else. Combining his geological knowledge with his understanding of how islands develop their own unique fauna, Darwin wondered whether the exotically different fauna of the Antipodes bore witness to the length of time the southern continent had been separated from other landmasses. According to notes made in 1837, he even realised that if so, the marsupials—or their ancestors—had become isolated at a time when no other mammals existed there![19]

Later in his life, Darwin would dramatically cross paths with another man who had been studying these same patterns and who was using them to argue for his own theory of the origins and evolution of species. He developed his theory in parallel with Darwin, though each was unaware of the other's interest in the subject. Born in Wales, Alfred Wallace came from a much less stable and privileged background than Darwin's. Only 12 years old when Darwin was sailing around the Galápagos, he was largely self-taught: his parents were able to afford only a few years' schooling for him before apprenticing him to a land surveyor at the age of 14. But Wallace was bitten by the beetle-collecting bug and longed to become a naturalist and an explorer. In 1848, he set off on his first major expedition, to Brazil, hoping to support himself by collecting specimens and selling them in Europe. Wallace spent four years in the vicinity of the Rio Negro, noticing that the wide Amazonian rivers were effective barriers to the spreading of certain mammalian species. Some monkeys were found only on one side of the river, some only on the other. However, nearer the headwaters, where the rivers were narrow enough to cross, there was a mixture of species—so it wasn't that they couldn't coexist.

Wallace spent his thirties in Malaysia and Indonesia, where again he observed marked differences in plant and animal distributions in neighbouring regions. In particular, he discovered a striking difference between the fauna on the islands closest to Malaysia and on those closest to New Guinea and Australia. Two entirely different sets of animals were found on adjacent islands separated at some points by as little as 20 miles. Wallace marked the distributions on a map and drew a line to demarcate the changeover. To the west of the line were well-known Asiatic mammals such as monkeys, rhinoceroses, and tigers; to the east were marsupials such as kangaroos, tree kangaroos, and opossums. "I believe the western part to be a separated portion of continental Asia", he wrote in an 1858 letter, "the eastern [to be] the fragmentary prolongation of a former Pacific continent.[20]

This line is known today as the Wallace line in recognition of his pioneering work in the field now known as biogeography. Wallace himself was basically content to note that the demarcation existed, without being able to explain how it came about. At that time, there was no scientific explanation of how continents now separated could previously have been joined together. According to the most popular account, there had been links between continents (and between continents and islands) in the form of land bridges. These eventually sank into the sea, but their flora and fauna—which the different geographical areas still shared in common—showed that the bridges had once been there.

Wallace died in 1913 at the ripe old age of 90; had he lived just a few years longer, he would have heard of a new theory that would have helped him explain the line. In 1915, Alfred Wegener published *The Origin of Continents and Oceans*, in which he advanced the idea of continental drift: he proposed that all continents were originally part of a single supercontinent, which he later called Pangaea. It has since revolutionised our understanding of the Earth and has contributed to the solution of many previously baffling problems regarding the geographical distribution of flora and fauna.

Innovative thinkers often go unrecognised by their contemporaries, and such was Wegener's fate. More or less ridiculed by his fellow scientists, he consequently had difficulty in securing academic positions. One problem was that he could propose no mechanism to explain continental drift. As a result, his idea became generally accepted only in the 1960s—after the discovery of plate tectonics, by which time Wegener had died on an expedition to the Greenland icecap.

We now know that Wegener was right about Pangaea. The gradual break-up of the supercontinent from the Jurassic period onwards explains the problem that Darwin was puzzling over: namely, why there are no mammals in Australia and no sloths outside South America? Simply put, both groups evolved *after* their home continents had split off from Pangaea. As Darwin was beginning to suspect, the distribution of animals and plants we see today is due to the history of their radiation from the place where they had their origins.

Darwin realised that he needed to find a mechanism by which such radiation or dissemination could take place. How did plants and animals actually get to remote islands? To this end, he concocted a series of simple experiments to see how possible it was for seeds to be spread over long distances. Cabbages and radishes failed to survive 14 days in salt water, but cress, spinach, oats, and barley all sprouted![21] Some species, such as celery and onions, could even tolerate lying in salt water for several months and still sprout. Darwin's American colleague Asa Gray, with whom he regularly corresponded, endorsed this discovery: "Why has nobody thought of trying the experiment before! instead of taking it for granted that salt water kills seeds".[22] Another colleague suggested a large-scale study of all possible seeds, but Darwin was not interested. It didn't matter which seeds survived, or where—for his purposes, the point was that sea-borne distribution was possible.[23]

CHAPTER 5

So similar, yet so different

THE *BEAGLE* LEFT the Galápagos in 1835, but nearly another entire year would pass before Darwin would arrive home, for on the way they would visit Tahiti, Polynesia, Australia, and South Africa. Even then, it was not over: after leaving South Africa, FitzRoy decided he needed to return to Brazil again to check some of his measurements, a decision which drove Darwin nearly to despair. The voyage had been long enough already. After two additional weeks of taking soundings off Brazil, FitzRoy was finally satisfied, and on October 2, 1836, the *Beagle* at last sailed into an English harbour. Its first port of call was Falmouth, in Cornwall. Darwin packed some essentials and disembarked at the first opportunity, longing to get back to his family as well as to be on dry land again; the *Beagle* continued to sail slowly up the English Channel towards London.

The journey back to Shrewsbury by horse-drawn mail-coach took two days, and by the time Darwin arrived, late in the evening, everyone had gone to bed. He did the same, waiting until breakfast time to surprise everyone with his return.[1] There was general delight, and his sister Catherine noted with satisfaction that the final stormy passage through the Bay of Biscay had only confirmed Darwin's dislike of sea travel. Hopefully, he would not soon be setting off on any more long voyages. Catherine's confidence was even better founded than she could anticipate: in fact, Darwin would never again leave England's shores.

For now, Darwin was happy to be home. He spent the next few weeks in a flurry of visits and dinner parties but soon had to face the classic conflict between family and career. He understood that his observations, and especially his collections of specimens, were his chance to make his name as a natural historian and scientist and that success would depend to a great degree on striking while the iron was hot. So, quite soon after his return, he was off to London to arrange for taking care of his crates of specimens. Apart from the ones he had sent to Henslow in advance, these were all still on board the *Beagle*, and Darwin wanted to be there when the ship docked and unloaded.

Darwin had already agreed with FitzRoy that his diaries of the voyage should be published along with FitzRoy's own travel journals, but the comprehensive collections of specimens he had amassed also needed to be examined and recorded. While awaiting the *Beagle*'s arrival, he hurried between Cambridge and London, trying to persuade suitable experts in the various fields to take on these tasks. Darwin himself would be the overall editor of whatever was published.

Some of these experts were carefully selected (for example, Richard Owen, who was eager to describe the fossil bones from Punta Alta and Monte Hermoso) while others were chosen perhaps more casually. Finding competent specialists willing to go through his finds was actually not so easy as Darwin had hoped. All the London museums were already full of a backlog of unopened crates shipped back from the four corners of the world. Apart from Lyell and Owen, he had met hardly anyone interested in his animal specimens. He wrote to Henslow at this time: "I see it is quite unreasonable to hope for a minute, that any man will undertake the examination of an whole order.— It is clear the collectors so much outnumber the real naturalists, that the latter have no time to spare".[2]

At the museum of the Zoological Society of London, however, Darwin found John Gould, who was interested in the birds and agreed to take a look at them. Darwin himself was no bird expert— his main interest, both before and during the voyage of the *Beagle*, was in shooting them for sport or for the pot. Still, he made an effort to put names to the birds he passed on to Gould. Amongst the collections he handed over was a bundle of unprepossessing, dark brown and black songbirds from the Galápagos. The labels read "warbler", "wren", "blackbird", and "some kind of grosbeak".

The Galápagos finches

Gould, a self-taught taxidermist, had become the first "Curator and Preserver" of the Zoological Society on its founding. The son of a gardener and with no formal education at all, he was nevertheless an expert ornithologist, and it didn't take him long to recognise that there were no grosbeaks, blackbirds, or warblers amongst Darwin's birds. They were all finches—each somewhat different in appearance, especially in regard to the shapes of their beaks, but nonetheless finches. Moreover, Gould announced to the amazed Darwin, the mockingbirds from the various islands were each a separate species and not just variants of a single species, as Darwin had assumed.

"I wonder if Darwin can say, which islands all these different finches are from?" one can almost hear Gould asking. That he could not do, unfortunately: Darwin, normally so meticulous, hadn't bothered to record such details—which must have been highly embarrassing for him to admit. Luckily, others on board the *Beagle* had not been so careless. FitzRoy and his steward Fuller, as well as Darwin's own servant Covington, had all gathered their own private collections in the

Galápagos and had kept good records of provenance. Darwin was able to borrow their specimens and compare them with his own.[3] Gould could then confirm that some very interesting patterns had emerged.

To start with, most of the birds Darwin had collected in the Galápagos were entirely new species, not known from anywhere else in the world. The four mockingbirds (which Darwin had scrutinised on board the *Beagle* and suspected were two varieties of the same species) turned out to represent three different species from three different islands. A fifth mockingbird, which Darwin had taken for a double of one of the species already collected, was yet another separate species.

In all, no fewer than 13 species of finches were represented in the collections from the *Beagle*. Three were ground-living species: one with a large, one with a medium-sized, and one with a small beak. Two finches with different-sized beaks were cactus-eaters. Then there were the tree-dwelling finches, again with three different beak sizes, as well as a large-beaked finch which lived off leaves and buds. One finch used its large beak to manipulate cactus thorns as tools, while another lived mainly in mangrove swamps. Finally, there were two warbler-sized finches with small, pointed beaks.

Perhaps the biggest surprise for Darwin was that both the mockingbirds and the finches had close relatives on the South American mainland. That certainly didn't fit the idea of the Galápagos as a "centre of creation". Many of the strange and wonderful animals and plants Darwin saw in the Galápagos Islands—for example, marine iguanas, giant tortoises, and scalesias (small trees belonging to the daisy family)—fit nicely with the theory that they were created just for this location and would not be found anywhere else. However, if that was how evolution worked, then the same should apply to the mockingbirds and finches—and yet clearly it did not.

Even though the finches may not have impressed Darwin when he saw them on the islands, it gradually dawned on him that they could be key to understanding how species evolved. In the first version of his travel journals, published in 1839, he was not yet ready to go so far, however—merely commenting: "I very much suspect, that certain members of the series are confined to different islands; therefore, if the collection had been made on any one island, it would not have presented so perfect a gradation." This sounds like an interesting beginning, but then Darwin immediately steps back without mentioning the implications—with what surely has to be the worst excuse ever in a book of 600 pages. "But there is not space in this work, to enter on this curious subject."[4] In truth, Darwin probably did not yet have enough evidence in place to put forward his theory of evolution at this early stage.

In 1845, in a new edition of his journal, he was slightly bolder. The question of which islands the various finches came from was no longer central. By now, Darwin had connected the finches' many different types of beak with their different foraging strategies. "The most curious fact is the perfect gradation in the size of the beaks in the different species of *Geospiza*, from one as large as that of a hawfinch to that of a chaffinch, and … even to that of a warbler … Seeing this gradation and diversity of structure in one small, intimately related group of birds, one might really fancy that from an original paucity of birds in this archipelago, one species had been taken and modified for different ends."[5]

The concept of 'species'

So, what exactly is a species? Most of us have a fairly intuitive grasp of the concept: an elephant is an elephant, and a corn poppy is a corn poppy. It sounds simple enough, but actually we're already in trouble with the elephant. Although it may seem easy to recognise an African elephant, there are actually several types. The much smaller forest elephants have long been categorised as a subspecies; they also have longer, more slender tusks and more rounded ears than the savannah elephant. Recently, however, American and Kenyan researchers have gone into dense rainforests and taken blood samples for DNA testing. The results show that the genetic differences between the two types of elephant are so great that it's reasonable to consider them as two separate species.[6]

Another good example of two species which look very similar is provided by the chiff-chaff and the willow warbler. Even if you hold them both in the hand (something not many people get to do!), they look almost identical. However, if you hear their songs, there is no doubt which is which. The opposite can also hold true: the same species can take many forms, and we need look no further than humans to confirm this. Human beings from different parts of the world can look very different with regard to skin and hair colour, stature and facial characteristics, but we all belong to the same species. Males and females of the same species can also look very different, so much so that they may be taken for two different species. This was the case when natural historians first classified male and female sperm whales—not surprisingly, since the males are more than twice the size of the females and the two sexes spend most of their lives far apart from each other.[7]

Natural historians, taxonomists, and biologists have struggled to separate and define species ever since the first attempts to systematise nature, and they have experimented with several definitions of what a species is. The most commonly used definition today was proposed by the renowned German evolutionary biologist Ernst Mayr in 1942: if two organisms can produce fertile offspring, they belong to the same species.[8] This is a sound definition, or at least one which is applicable in most situations, although it must be said that it is more usable with animals than with plants, fungi or bacteria. We can use it to determine that all domesticated dogs belong to the same species, however different their appearances and even though we most likely would never see a cross between a dachshund and a Great Dane. Lions and tigers, however, are a different story. In the wild, they rarely have occasion to mate; but when confined together in a zoo, they will occasionally mate and sometimes produce young. However, any offspring surviving to maturity are always sterile, therefore lions and tigers belong to different species. Similarly, the progeny of a horse and a donkey—either a mule or a hinny—might be useful beasts of burden, but they are no good for breeding purposes. It is a different matter with plants; many plants hybridize and some produce fertile offspring, which complicate matters when trying to sort out which species is which.

It's important for any animal to find a mate of the right species; otherwise, its mating is a waste of time in terms of passing on one's genes to the next generation. Animals (and plants as well) have developed a wealth of mechanisms to ensure that they can recognise the right species to breed with. With animals, it's often olfactory, aural, or visual signals which announce to conspecifics that this is a potential mate. With plants, it's the specialised adaptations to specific pollinators—whether ants, bats, bees, bumblebees, or hummingbirds—which serve the same purpose in guaranteeing effective fertilisation.

Darwin was very concerned with the problem of differentiating between species, not least because of a letter he received in February 1846 from one of his closest friends and colleagues, Joseph Hooker. Darwin had gotten to know Hooker while searching for a handy botanist to examine the plants brought back to England. The young Hooker was both well travelled and a keen plant expert, thanks to his upbringing at the feet of his father, then England's leading botanist and director of the Royal Botanical Gardens at Kew. (Joseph Hooker would follow in his father's footsteps in both regards later in life.) He had eagerly accepted Darwin's proposal to work on the plant collections from the *Beagle* journey, and a warm and life-long friendship soon developed. They corresponded regularly and at length, mostly on botanical matters, but in time also on more personal subjects.

At one point, in discussing the characteristic flora of volcanic islands, Hooker dismissed the thinking of a French colleague on the grounds that, even though the Frenchman was a competent physiologist and a very nice man, it was difficult to take his opinions on plant taxonomy seriously because he was "not a systematist".[9] Darwin felt Hooker's remark as a body blow, although it was certainly not meant as such. The French colleague was not the only one who had not studied taxonomic systematics in detail, Darwin realised. He himself had read widely and travelled far, but he had no solid background in the classification of species. This letter seems to have been a factor in Darwin's decision to throw himself into the study of a small, unnoticed group of animals whose systematics were as yet poorly defined: marine barnacles, These animals superficially resemble molluscs such as mussels but are actually arthropods, more closely related to crabs and lobsters, and their study would occupy Darwin for more than eight years. He reasoned that by the time he would finally publish his ideas about the evolution of species—having studied barnacles in such detail—nobody would be able to say he didn't know what a species was.

At the outset of his studies, Darwin surely had no idea how absorbed in his barnacles he would become. But the long hours spent toiling away at dissecting thousands of these tiny creatures under a microscope would prove well worth it. By the time he published his four-volume monograph *Cirrepedia*, he had hands-on practical experience and detailed theoretical understanding of the latest developments in the emerging field of systematics. Moreover, Darwin's last word on barnacles, still a valuable work of reference today, received very favourable reviews in the scientific press and cemented his reputation as a serious man of science—not just an amateur.

Variability of species

Examining and comparing his barnacle specimens also gave Darwin several key insights into factors affecting the evolution of species in general. One problem he came up against, and not for the first time, was intraspecific variation. "I have been struck", he wrote to Hooker, "with the variability of every part in some slight degree of every species: when the same organ is rigorously compared in many individuals I always find some slight variability, & consequently that the diagnosis of species from minute differences is always dangerous".[10]

The recognition that there is variation at every level between members of the same species became an important piece in the jigsaw puzzle Darwin was building to account for the origin of species. During his own lifetime, it would not be possible to explain quite how variations arose, but that they did so was clear enough. No two oak trees are alike, every snail shell is different, even earthworms are unique if you look closely. Anyone who has children or siblings can easily observe that, even with the same parents, there are great variations amongst the offspring. Some will be taller or shorter, some more solidly built or more slender; some will have blue eyes and others brown; some will love maths problems; and others will have fine singing voices.

How can so much variation arise when the parents are the same? One explanation is obvious: not all characteristics which vary can be attributed to inheritance, for upbringing must undoubtedly also play a part. For example, height and weight depend to some extent on living conditions, including the amount of food consumption.

However, the same cannot be said of eye colour or any other characteristics which we inherit from our parents and which do not depend on our upbringing. If siblings do not inherit exactly the same traits from the same parents, then the genetic content of each egg cell or sperm cell must differ from that of other cells and from the parents' cells.

Thanks to work done towards the end of the 19th century, we know now that egg and sperm cells (gametes) are produced by means of a special process of cell division called meiosis. Chromosomes, which are normally found in pairs—and which carry the genetic instructions for how an organism will develop—separate into two sets during this process. This means that sex cells or gametes include only one of each chromosome pair. So when they join together with their opposite numbers from the other parent during fertilisation, the normal number of chromosomes is restored, while genetic material from both parents contributes to the makeup of the offspring. However, there is more to sexual reproduction than that. In the initial phase of meiosis, the string-like chromosomes come together in pairs, often crossing over each other at certain points. At these points, they may swap sections; thus a piece of chromosome on one string can be exchanged with a piece of a similar chromosome on the other string. Crossing over means that the chromosomes of the sex cells in a sexually reproducing organism are already different from the chromosomes in all the other cells of its body. These so-called "recombined" chromosomes contain new and unique combinations of genes, which is the source of genetic variation. Without this process, all children of the same parents would be genetically identical. When fertilisation takes place, the chromosomes from each parent—each including some recombined chromosomes where crossing over took place—pair up again to form the genetic blueprint for a unique new individual with a unique genetic composition.

Darwin cultivates his contacts

In March 1837, Darwin moved to London, where he was happy to be in the thick of the scientific goings-on in the capital. Most men of science of this era were gentlemen of independent means, benefiting from a private income rather than having to work for a living. There was a certain tendency to look down on those natural historians who had to supplement their income with jobs at a museum or university in order to survive. Luckily, Darwin was one of the fortunate ones who never needed to stoop to this drudgery, as his family fortune sufficed to allow him to devote himself to his studies without having to worry about money.

Now a celebrated man of the world, Darwin was constantly invited to dinner parties and get-togethers with like-minded individuals. Lyell introduced him to anyone worth knowing, and he was soon elected to both the Geological Society and the Athenaeum, both gentlemen's clubs of their own kind. Members' clubs such as the Athenaeum boasted stylish dining rooms, comfortable drawing rooms, and well-stocked libraries. They were popular retreats for upper-class men to read the daily newspapers or have lunch—naturally without the troublesome distraction of any females being present. Above all, though, they were places for meeting friends and making new contacts within the more influential circles. Most members of the Athenaeum were there by virtue of inherited titles and positions, but the club was also known for its strong bias towards the arts and sciences and for admitting men who had achieved prominence through their intellectual influence and achievements.

Darwin took to this experience of privilege with enthusiasm, reporting happily to Lyell: "After the second half day is finished, I go & dine at the Athenæum like a gentleman, or rather like a Lord, for I am sure the first evening I sat in that great drawing room, all on a sofa by myself, I felt just like a duke.—I am full of admiration at the

Athenæum; one meets so many people there, that one likes to see.—
The very first time I dined there, (i.e., last week) I met Dr Fitton at
the door & he got together quite a party, Robert Brown (who is gone
to Paris & Auvergne) Macleay & Dr Boot."[11]

Eventually, Darwin managed to dispose of most of his collections.
Owen was already working on the fossils and Gould on the birds.
Leonard Jenyns, another Cambridge naturalist and former protégé of
Henslow's, took the fish. Jenyns was probably especially interested in
examining the collection, as it was he who had first received the offer
of being the naturalist on board the *Beagle*, which he turned down.
The mammals were passed to George Waterhouse, one of Gould's
colleagues from the Zoological Society, while Thomas Bell, professor
of zoology at King's College, London, took the reptiles. With all his
finds distributed amongst the experts who would help him to describe them, Darwin could concentrate on his role as editor. He also
could polish his travel diaries, which were to be published along with
FitzRoy's account of the *Beagle*'s voyage.

But there was one small matter to take care of first. Darwin was
now 29 years old—and still unmarried.

CHAPTER 6

Better than a dog

THE QUESTION OF marriage had certainly crossed Darwin's mind before. In July 1838, he decided to tackle it in his usual, thoroughly rational way. He sat down with a blank sheet of paper, wrote at the top, "This is the question", and drew two columns: "Marry" and "Not marry". On the left side, he listed the advantages and disadvantages of marrying; on the right side, the advantages and disadvantages of remaining single.[1] His columns soon became muddled, but maybe it did bring some rationality to his decision after all!

Marry
Children — (if it Please God) — Constant companion (& friend in old age) who will feel interested in one — object to be beloved & played with — better than a dog, anyhow. — Home, & someone to take care of house — Charms of music & female chit-chat. — These things good for one's health. — Forced to visit and receive relations but terrible loss of time.

My God, it is intolerable to think of spending one's whole life, like a neuter bee, working, working, & nothing after all. — No, no won't do. — Imagine living all one's day solitarily in smoky dirty London House. — Only picture to yourself a nice soft wife on a sofa with good fire, & books &

music perhaps — Compare this vision with the dingy reality of Grt. Marlbro' St.

He finished this column with the words: Marry — Mary — Marry Q.E.D.

In the next column, he wrote down the consequences of not marrying.

Not Marry
No children (no second life), no one to care for one in old age. — What is the use of working without sympathy from near and dear friends — Who are near and dear friends to the old except relatives. — Freedom to go where one liked — Choice of Society & little of it. — Conversation of clever men at clubs — Not forced to visit relatives, & to bend in every trifle. — To have the expense & anxiety of children — perhaps quarrelling — Loss of time. — cannot read in the Evenings — fatness & idleness — Anxiety & responsibility — less money for books &c — if many children, forced to gain one's bread. — (But then, it is very bad for one's health to work too much)

Perhaps my wife won't like London; then the sentence is banishment & degradation into indolent, idle fool.

The balance of pros and cons was clear, to Darwin at least: he must marry. The next question was whether this should be sooner or later, and a similar analysis on the back side of the same piece of paper did express some regrets about the loss of freedom which marriage would entail: "Eheu!! I never should know French,—or see the Continent,— or go to America, or go up in a Balloon", he groaned. Still, the conclusion was clear enough: he must get on with the business, or it would be too late to have children, as his father had warned him. Darwin consoled himself accordingly: "Never mind, my boy—Cheer up—One cannot live this solitary life, with groggy old age, friendless and cold and childless staring one in one's face, already beginning to wrinkle ... trust to chance — keep a sharp look out — There is many a happy slave —"[2]

So that was that. Now it was just a matter of finding the wife. Darwin looked around his circle of friends and acquaintances and made another rapid decision. A few months after the jottings on the piece of paper, he proposed to his cousin, Emma. She was the daughter of his uncle, Josiah Wedgwood, and they had known each other all their lives; the two families were very close. It was Uncle Jos who had spoken up for Charles when his own father was putting the brakes on his idea of joining the *Beagle* voyage, something Darwin had not forgotten. Marriage between first cousins was not uncommon in well-to-do Victorian families; in fact, Darwin's own parents were cousins. An advantage of such marriages was that they helped to keep money within the family, and in Charles and Emma's case there was money on both branches of the family tree. Robert Darwin was already a very wealthy man, having married a Wedgwood himself, but his assets were modest compared with the still-growing Wedgwood family fortune, founded on the china-manufacturing business.

Emma Wedgwood, the youngest of seven, was already 30 when she accepted Darwin's proposal. She was surely aware that at her age, she risked leaving it too late to find a husband at all. This may have encouraged her to say yes to Darwin, but theirs would nevertheless become a strong and loving bond. Like the rest of the Wedgwood family, she took her Unitarian faith very seriously, and Darwin's father warned him to handle religious questions carefully with Emma.

Although Darwin had previously considered the life of a country parson for himself, and continued to count himself a believer, he had also begun to nurture doubts. He may not have abandoned his Christian faith entirely, but neither was it at all solid—particularly with regard to the literal truth of the Bible. Years later, recalling his father's advice at the time, he wrote: "Before I was engaged to be married, my father advised me to conceal carefully my doubts, for he said that he had known extreme misery thus caused with married persons. Things went on pretty well until the wife or husband became out of health, and then some women suffered miserably by doubting about the salvation of their husbands, thus making them likewise to suffer".[3] Darwin was not given to such concealment, however; he ignored the advice and shared his doubts with Emma, which did indeed cause her to worry, just as predicted.

The wedding took place the following January and was a modest affair, the honeymoon even more so. In fact, it consisted solely of a train journey back to London from Maer in Staffordshire, the Wedgwood family seat. Emma and Charles shared sandwiches and a bottle of water on the train, and in this frugal way their marriage began.[4] In London, they moved into the small house in Gower Street which Darwin had rented at the turn of the year, and which they christened "Macaw Cottage". The recently discovered synthetic dyes were all the rage, and the previous owner had painted all the walls and furniture in vivid yellows, reds, and blues.

Malthus

At the same time that Darwin was considering the pros and cons of marriage, he acquired a book about which he had already heard much talk. Thomas Malthus' *Essay on the Principle of Population* was the first work to discuss in depth the consequences for economic development of a growing population. At this time, England was experiencing considerable social unrest, which—according to Malthus—was not hard to understand. He calculated that a human population could double in 20 years, were it not for losses due to starvation, disease, and war holding the growth in check. He regarded price increases and low wages as natural consequences of the growth of population and the resultant competition for food and other resources. Malthus did not restrict his thesis to human society but also drew parallels to the natural world: "Through the animal and vegetable kingdoms, nature has scattered the seeds of life abroad with the most profuse and liberal hand. She has been comparatively sparing in the room and the nourishment necessary to rear them".[5] If the Earth had not become overpopulated with human beings, or any other single species of animal or plant (for some unfathomable reason, Malthus mentioned fennel as an example), it was because there would always be a struggle for resources—and in such a struggle, there would always be winners and losers.

If you live in a suburban area, you may be able to observe this phenomenon for yourself. In a normal season, common garden birds such as blackbirds typically manage to raise three clutches, each consisting of four chicks on average. That means about 12 new blackbirds in the garden after an average summer. If these all survived the winter and succeeded in attracting a mate and reproducing at the same rate, there would be 156 blackbirds in the garden by the end of next year! However, what we actually tend to observe is that next summer, there are just the usual two blackbirds in the garden, often still using the same nest as last year. What happened to all the young they produced? In this example, it's highly likely that of the 12 chicks, one never flew the nest because it was a runt and never got as much food as its stronger siblings. Two of the chicks were caught by the neighbour's cat while still learning to fly; an additional one was seized by a magpie and another by a sparrowhawk. Two died of hunger during the autumn because they were not good enough at finding food, and before Christmas another juvenile was hit by a car while flying over the road. During the winter, one of the young birds died of a bacterial infection and two more starved to death when frost and snow made it even harder to find food. When spring arrived, only one of the 12 had survived. Meanwhile, the male blackbird in the original pair had died, so the total number of blackbirds in the garden was still only two.

Wherever we look, there is a surplus of seeds, eggs, and babies in the world. An oak tree can produce 2,000 acorns in a year and live for more than 500 years. That could mean millions of new oak trees in just a few years, but it doesn't—because most acorns don't last long enough to become fruit-bearing trees. Most acorns are eaten by squirrels, mice, and jays and never even manage to germinate. Those that land beneath the parent trees rarely grow more than a few inches tall: they are shaded and starved of water and nutrients by the already established root systems of the bigger trees. Only those few acorns which birds and rodents drop by accident at a distance from the parent tree, or bury and then forget, have a reasonable chance of growing up to become one of the forest giants.

Two different strategies

Broadly speaking, animals have two basic strategies with regard to procreating the species. One is to produce only a few young every year—or sometimes even less frequently—but to take good care of them. Elephants, for example, have only one baby at a time and several years apart. Pregnancy is long, and the young are dependent on the mother for a long time as well; however, survival rates to adulthood are very high. The opposite strategy, to have lots of young and invest less care in each of them, accepts high mortality but assumes that one or two will make it through in any case. Mice, for example, have large litters several times a year, with short pregnancies and rapid weaning of the young; yet the result is approximately the same in terms of how many adults survive to reproduce. Plants operate on the same principles. Either they set a lot of seeds (most of which get eaten, fall on unsuitable ground, or otherwise fail—like the oak seedlings already mentioned), or they invest in relatively few seeds but supply them with plentiful resources so they have a better chance of surviving, sprouting, and growing to maturity—like the coconut palm.

Even with species producing enormous numbers of offspring, there is not necessarily any increased risk of the Earth's being taken over by these species. The sunfish, for example, produces more eggs than any other vertebrate (up to 300 million in a single spawning) but is still a relatively rare animal. Presumably, nearly all the eggs are lost before they even get fertilised; many marine animals specialise in eating fish eggs and larvae, and for them the sunfish roe is an important food resource. The end result is the same as with blackbirds: most progeny do not survive to reproduce, and most populations remain roughly constant.

Despite such different reproductive strategies, most plant and animal populations are still fairly stable in the natural world. There can be upswings and downswings, but dramatic and long-lasting changes are rare.

When the krill disappeared

It is a different situation, however, when a key species within an ecosystem is removed. In the 19th century and in the first half of the 20th century, fur seals and then the great whales of the Antarctic region were hunted extensively. Norwegian and Russian whalers focused especially on blue whales and fin whales towards the end of this period: it is estimated that less than one percent of the original populations of these species remained when the factory ships withdrew in the 1960s. Because fur seals and great whales live mainly off the small crustaceans known as krill, their removal from the food chain over a period of 200 years led to an explosion in the numbers of krill. Scientists have discussed for years what effect this may have had on other species in the ecosystem. Is it a coincidence that the numbers of crabeater seals in the Antarctic are now so large that they are thought to be one of the most numerous large mammal species on the planet?

Despite their name, crabeater seals do not eat crabs but rather krill, so when the fur seals and great whales disappeared, the seals had the chance to exploit a resource for which there would previously have been strong competition. We have no accurate population figures for crabeater seals—either before the whales were virtually wiped out in the region or at the present time—and there may be other factors besides food availability which contributed to their recent success, but the krill story is surely a key factor.

One thing is certain: more krill have been available in the Antarctic ecosystem since the decimation of the whales and fur seals. In one species at least—the Adélie penguin—we are sure that this has led to a complete change of diet. Steven Emslie of the University of North Carolina and William Patterson of the University of Saskatchewan have analysed egg shells of the Adélie penguin to determine the amounts of certain carbon and nitrogen isotopes present. Because these isotopes are derived from the penguins' food, and because we know that fish contain higher proportions of C-13 and N-15 than does krill, it is possible to deduce what the penguins have been eating based on the proportion of these isotopes in their shells. Emslie and Patterson collected eggshells from current and historic Antarctic nesting sites, where shells are well preserved in the cold and dry conditions, amassing a data series going back in time as far as 38,000 years. The isotope compositions left no doubt that sometime within the past 200 years, the penguins had transitioned from a diet consisting exclusively of fish to one consisting exclusively of krill.[6]

A nice twist to this story is that the researchers obtained permission to analyse eggshells from the hut of explorer Captain Robert F. Scott at Cape Evans, in order to get a closer fix on when the shift from fish to krill took place. The hut had been used only a couple of times after Scott's tragic death on his return from the South Pole, so the eggs could be dated accurately to no later than 1917. With this evidence, Emslie and Patterson showed that the shift from fish to krill had already taken place at this point in time.

Another piece

Reading Malthus was another crucial piece in Darwin's jigsaw puzzle of the origin of species. When every species continually lays more eggs, produces more seeds, or has more young than can possibly survive, a struggle for survival ensues, both among species and—just as importantly—between conspecifics. Darwin realised that it was not simply a matter of chance which ones survived and which ones fell by the wayside. On the contrary, the survivors must have some qualities which distinguish them from those who die. Most important, they need qualities enabling them to survive long enough to reproduce. If a blackbird, oak tree, or human being succeeds in producing more offspring—which survive to reproduce more than its fellows within the species do—then over generations, there will be more of just that kind of blackbird or oak tree in the population.

Darwin moves to the country

In 1842, Darwin and Emma—now with two children and another on the way—moved to the country. London was by that time already the largest city in the world; then as now, it was noisy and dirty, and economic growth had brought with it great inequalities of wealth and social unrest. The Darwins both longed for a more peaceful life, and Charles's health was already uncertain. He was no longer comfortable with being in society, finding that he was better disposed when he could work quietly and undisturbed by visitors. He and Emma found a place to settle in the small village of Downe in rural Kent, two hours' drive (by horse-drawn coach!) from the city. The property they bought, Down House, had plenty of space for their growing family: there was a large room, ideal for Darwin's study, as well as a drawing room, dining room, and plenty of bedrooms. A large open garden fronted onto a small copse and the surrounding meadows. Here Darwin would live for the rest of his life, only occasionally travelling further than the nearby village.

In the garden of Down House, Darwin carried out practical experiments concerning the competition between species. He cleared an area of all vegetation and sowed a selection of seeds to see what would happen. Later, he reported the results to his friend Hooker: "My observations, though on so infinitely a small scale, on the struggle for existence, begin to make me see a little clearer how the fight goes on: out of 16 kinds of seed sown on my meadow, 15 have germinated, but now they are perishing at such a rate that I doubt whether more than one will flower".[7]

On a visit to Moor Park in Surrey, where a common had recently been enclosed, Darwin observed that young trees were "springing up by the millions, looking exactly as if planted, so many are of same age", while in the neighbouring unenclosed heathland, still grazed by cattle, "I looked for miles & not one young tree cd be seen; I then went near ... & looked closely in the heather, & there I found tens of thousands of young scotch-firs (30 in one square yard) with their tops nibbled off by the few cattle which occasionally roam over these wretched Heaths. One little tree three inches high, by the rings appeared to be 26 years old with a short stem about as thick as stick of sealing wax."[8]

"What a wondrous problem it is," he wrote excitedly to Hooker, "what a play of forces, determining the kinds & proportions of each plant in a square yard of turf! It is to my mind truly wonderful ...". In the same letter, Darwin enumerated all the weeds which had sprouted in a patch of ground he had reserved for this purpose. Of the 357 plants which had grown on this patch, 277 had been eaten by snails and slugs! Yes, the struggle for survival was going on everywhere, even on the lawns of Down House.

Darwin's private life was also a struggle. The marriage with Emma was a happy one; a new baby arrived approximately every other year (ten would be born in total, of which seven would survive to adulthood), and the love and affection between the couple continued to grow. But Darwin's health was not what it had been. He suffered from dizziness, heart palpitations, indigestion and flatulence, sickness and vomiting; he got frequent headaches and was often anxious and depressed. For long periods of time, his poor health prevented him from working at all, which was very frustrating for him and led him to seek advice and treatment from numerous doctors, to little avail. None could give him a clear diagnosis; his symptoms were mysterious and non-specific, and some doctors thought his problem was purely nervous in origin. He was reluctant to leave Down House, and definitely not without Emma by his side. At times, Darwin put his work aside and the entire family travelled to spas such as Malvern, where he tried the latest cures. One such cure, which involved being wrapped in cold, wet towels every day, did seem to help, strangely enough— but only for a while. Soon the heart palpitations, sickness, and vomiting returned to plague him again.

Darwin's unexplained ailments, which severely impacted the last 40 years of his life, have been much discussed in light of modern advances in medical understanding—but without arriving at any definite conclusions. One theory is that he had caught Chagas disease, caused by a tropical protozoan parasite. We know that Darwin was bitten by the insects (known as "kissing bugs"), which are vectors for this parasite, during the voyage of the *Beagle*. Others are more inclined to see his illnesses as psychosomatic, since they clearly got worse when he was under the strain of working too much.

Rest, peace, and loving care helped him most. Emma's role as nursemaid and caregiver to her growing flock of children increasingly expanded to include tending to her sick husband as the foremost of her charges. Luckily, she accepted this duty willingly. During their engagement, she already had had a warning of what lay ahead when Darwin apologised in a letter for not feeling well. Emma responded warmly: "... nothing could make me so happy as to feel that I could be of any use or comfort to my own dear Charles when he is not well. ... So don't be ill any more my dear Charley, till I can be with you to nurse you & save you from bothers".[9]

CHAPTER 7

Laws of life

BY THE LATE 1830s, Darwin had all the pieces he would need to complete the puzzle of the origin and development of species. From Lyell he had learnt that tiny, gradual alterations could lead to enormous changes, if there was sufficient time available. The geological perspective had also shown him that Earth itself must be many, many millions of years old. He had himself found fossilised mussel shells high above sea level in the mountains of South America; he had experienced a powerful earthquake, demonstrating how geological uplift could change a landscape.

From Richard Owen's examination of the fossil animal bones Darwin had excavated in Punta Alta and Monte Hermoso, he knew that extinct species were often related to living species found in the same region.

The two species of rhea found in South America had taught him that closely related species could be found in adjacent parts of a larger region and not just in precisely the same area. He had seen that the greater rhea lived in the northern parts of South America, whereas the lesser rhea, the "avestruz petise", was found only in the southern part of the continent. Observations of the geographical distribution of other animals and plants confirmed this pattern. Darwin also knew that even though there was often an entirely unique flora and fauna on isolated islands, these island species were related to animals and plants on the mainland.

Darwin had recognised two further central facts after returning from the voyage of the *Beagle*. First, within each species there is almost endless variation. Second, most species produce a large excess of offspring, of which only a small number will survive to reproduce again. Finally, he also knew that many characteristics are inherited by children from their parents—and that the same applies in animals and plants. The question of inheritance was admittedly a fly in the ointment. He could see *that* it happened, but not *how*: the mechanism remained a mystery. For now, Darwin resolved to put that question aside; it was enough to know that characteristics were inherited from one generation to the next.

The transmutation notebooks

The overarching question which Darwin was gearing up to address was recorded in one of his notebooks: "The grand question which every naturalist ought to have before him when dissecting a whale or classifying a mite, a fungus, or an infusorian is, 'What are the Laws of Life?'"[1]. From 1837 to 1840, he filled a series of notebooks with observations, thoughts, and jottings related to the evolution of species—a process which he gradually convinced himself was real, although he couldn't yet go public with his conclusions.

Darwin's notebooks, labelled simply with the letters of the alphabet, have become an invaluable source for understanding the development of his thoughts and ideas. Notebooks B through E became known later as the transmutation notebooks—the contemporary term for what we would call "evolution". On the first page, he inscribed the heading "Zoonomia" in reference to his grandfather's book of that name. Now Darwin would complete the work which Erasmus had started. The notebooks reveal that the questions he was asking himself as his research continued ranged far and wide over biology, anthropology, and philosophy. Why do men have nipples? Why are there two types of rhea in South America? Why is life so short? Why do twins so resemble each other? And so on.[2] He was also interested in domesticated animals and cultivated plants, observing that they diverged in many ways from their wild forbears—as of course they were intended to by breeders who, over many generations, had carefully selected the stocks best suited for their purpose.

Darwin speculated as to how species could be related to each other and whether all species were linked by common lines of descent, noting that "Organised beings represent a tree irregularly branched".[3] Then again, some lines had come to a full stop, as he pondered a few pages later: "The tree of life should perhaps be called the coral of life, base of branches dead; so that passages cannot be seen".[4] On one momentous page, Darwin made a first quick sketch of how such a family tree of species could look, under the heading "I think". The drawing shows how a species-tree divides irregularly from a common ancestor and grows new branches, giving rise to new species. Some branches are more "bushy" than others, indicating the evolution of many new species, as we would say now. Others, however, end in a straight line, indicating that a species has gone extinct and no more development is possible in that direction.

Natural selection

Darwin continued to fill his notebooks with observations, thoughts, and ideas to be further explored. He posed questions that puzzled him. He no longer doubted that species changed and that over time, new species evolved; the key question was *how* this happened. It was here that the idea of the struggle for space and resources, which he had picked up from Malthus, proved useful. It happens all by itself, he realised, by means of a mechanism which he called "natural selection".

That evolution happens by itself without any preconceived plan, and that it is impossible to say which direction it will take, was possibly the most controversial aspect of Darwin's entire theory. The type and number of variations may be a matter of chance, but it is not accidental which of the many variations will survive. And not just "survive", but survive long enough for an organism to reproduce and pass the variations on. Considering how many people had speculated for so many years about the phenomenon of species—and their development, distribution on Earth, and extinction—the simplicity of Darwin's theory was striking. It was this very simplicity which caused Darwin's friend Huxley to strike himself on the forehead and exclaim, "How extremely stupid not to have thought of that!", when he first heard of the idea.

Darwin himself did not at first use the expression "survival of the fittest". It was coined by the English philosopher Herbert Spencer in his 1864 book *Principles of Biology*, which leaned heavily on Darwin's ideas. Unfortunately, the expression has often been misunderstood. By "fittest", Darwin did not mean the most athletic or the strongest, but rather the best fitted or best suited to environmental and other conditions of life. In modern parlance, we speak of the best "adapted". Again, natural selection is not about "survival" as such, let alone the survival of individuals. In order for the process to work, it suffices that some individuals have more surviving offspring than others and that the characteristics differentiating individuals are hereditary.

Darwin's explanation of evolution was fundamentally different from Lamarck's. To understand this, we return to Lamarck's example of the giraffe, who supposedly got his long neck by stretching to reach leaves higher in the tree tops. The giraffe would then have passed this trait on to his offspring—the inheritance of acquired characteristics. But according to Darwin's idea, of all the giraffes born, some would have necks slightly longer than average and would thus be able to utilise a food source not available to typical giraffes—namely, the leaves so high up that only a giraffe with a really long neck could reach them. If that extra resource caused those giraffes to grow up healthier and stronger—and, as a result, successfully produce more offspring (also with slightly longer necks) than their fellows with shorter necks, then natural selection would operate to "select" giraffes with slightly longer necks. Over many generations, the giraffe population as a whole would tend to develop longer necks, until the point where even longer necks would bring more problems than rewards. Meanwhile, lots of giraffes with shorter-than-average necks would also be born, but it is not they who will write evolutionary history. They will lose out in the competition for food resources and have fewer healthy offspring, so their trait of having short necks will quickly be "selected against".

Natural selection in everyday life

Maybe we don't often think about it, but we actually come across the processes of evolution and natural selection in many everyday situations. Any parents of children who have had head lice know how irritatingly difficult it is to get rid of these pests. Shampoo available at the chemist's might kill most of the lice, but not all of them; after a few weeks, they are back again in large numbers. A 2006 Danish study found that, after decades of exposure, the louse population now exhibits a high level of resistance to the most commonly used chemicals in lice shampoo—malathion and permethrin.[5] In some trials, 75 percent of lice survived treatment with these poisons. The ability of the lice to withstand a previously deadly chemical attack is due to a mutation in one of their genes. That mutation has perhaps always been present in a section of the louse population, without necessarily bringing any advantages or disadvantages. But when we started treating head lice with permethrin, lice with this protective gene suddenly had an advantage. And because their descendants thrived and survived, the gene is now more widespread in the population, as are more and more permethrin-resistant lice. Luckily, they are no more immune to patient and repeated treatment with a fine-toothed comb than their non-resistant cousins!

Similarly, bacteria have become resistant to antibiotics such as penicillin. When penicillin was discovered in the 1940s, it was a miracle cure. Previously fatal diseases such as pneumonia, tuberculosis, and blood poisoning, which killed many thousands, could now be cured relatively easily—at least in those with access to medicine. However, the more widely penicillin became used, the more bacterial mutations making them immune to penicillin were favoured; and so resistance spread. Hospitals worldwide are reporting increasing problems with diseases that used to be easy to cure with antibiotics. Multi-resistant bacteria are creating havoc, and people are dying from conditions which were easily remedied only a decade or so ago.

Milk and evolution

Another good example of natural selection, familiar from daily life for many of us, is the ability to digest milk as an adult. Most people in northern Europe manage this without much problem, but in southern Europe only 25 percent to 50 percent of the adult population can tolerate milk. In many other parts of the world, only children can digest milk. Symptoms of milk intolerance such as diarrhoea, stomach pain, nausea, and bloating are usually enough to make people give up milk and dairy products.

All children have the lactase enzyme in their gut, enabling them to break down lactose, the milk sugar found in all types of animal milk, including human milk. Normally, the ability to produce the enzyme disappears after weaning. In human populations that can tolerate dairy milk as adults, the body retains its ability to produce lactase throughout life. This "lactase persistence" has been traced to a mutation of the gene which regulates lactase production.[6]

It's not hard to imagine that the ability to digest milk would be an advantage in human populations living so far north that it was difficult to obtain enough food in winter. The extra food resource offered by milk from domestic animals in such societies could provide adults with access to such products—and the ability to make use of them—better nourishment than those who lacked it. Supplementing their diets with milk would limit their exposure to hunger and all hunger-diseases. As a result, such persons might be able to raise more children, who would then inherit the same ability to digest milk as adults. This trait would then have gradually spread throughout the population, and it seems to have spread rather rapidly. Considering that in biological terms, domestication of dairy animals is a relatively recent phenomenon, the lactase persistence gene is very widespread in Europe. The advantage it conferred on those who had it was so great that it spread like wildfire.

In most parts of Africa, the population cannot tolerate lactose as adults; however, especially in East Africa, there are tribes where milk is an important part of the diet and adults can digest it just as well as northern Europeans. These are tribes such as the Maasai in Kenya and the Beja in Sudan, where cattle herding is a vital part of the culture. Like most Europeans, these tribal peoples also carry a mutation in the gene controlling production of the enzyme lactase. However, it's not universally the same mutation. In fact, no fewer than three distinct mutations have been found in different African tribes—all having the same effect of maintaining lactase production into adulthood.[7] This means that we know of at least four separate occasions when a random mutation in this gene has conferred sufficiently favourable advantages for people in cattle-raising communities that it spread and was preserved.

Colour variations in the peppered moth

One of the earliest and most famous examples of the operation of natural selection was provided by the peppered moth *Biston betularia*. This common moth of temperate climates such as England occurs in both a light grey and an almost black variant. Before the Industrial Revolution, this latter melanistic form was extremely rare. The trees the moth rested on were pale-coloured and the lichen which grew on the trees was also pale. Thus the light-grey moth was much better camouflaged and therefore less likely to be eaten by birds. However, as coal-based industrial output increased, by the middle of the 19th century it was not just clothes on the washing line which were in danger of getting dirty from the soot and carbon particles being belched out by the nation's chimneys and furnaces. The surrounding woodlands were soon affected as well, with many trees coated in filth. At the same time, air pollution was killing the lichens, adding to the darkening effect.

The previously rare melanistic variant of the peppered moth began to turn up in more and more places. Only 50 years after first being recorded, it had already almost entirely replaced the lighter-coloured type in most industrialised areas. In fact, by 1896 it was suggested that this change was due to the moth's gradual adaptation to darker tree trunks. The dark variant was less visible on darker surfaces and so was better protected against birds and other predators.

In the 1950s, English biologist Bernard Kettlewell carried out a series of studies of the peppered moths. Following a common research procedure, he captured a sample of moths, marked them, and released them back into the wild in both polluted woodlands near Birmingham and unpolluted woodlands in Dorset. He later returned to sample the population again, to see how many of the marked moths were represented. These mark-and-recapture trials showed clearly that the pale variants survived better in the unpolluted areas characterised by pale, lichen-covered trees, while the dark variants did better in polluted woodlands with darker tree trunks.[8] The moths were thus confirmed as a good illustration of how natural selection can operate on a wild population, even over a very short time period.

Holes were later picked in Kettlewell's methods: he released the moths in daylight, whereas normally they fly at night; he put them onto tree trunks, whereas they actually prefer to be underneath small branches and twigs; and he used too few release sites, so the moths were too crowded. Critics also pointed out that bats, as well as birds, eat peppered moths—and they don't care what colour the moths are because they find them by echolocation. Michael Majerus, Professor of Evolution at Cambridge University, didn't agree with the criticism. He undertook a seven-year-long series of experiments in the 2000s, carefully avoiding all the pitfalls Kettlewell had supposedly fallen into—and more besides—and convincingly showing that any flaws in the original experiments had not affected the validity of the conclusions. The peppered moth was restored as one of the clearest examples of natural selection in action.[9]

Majerus completed his work only just in time. In the aftermath of clean-air legislation introduced in England from the 1950s onwards, tree trunks have become paler again and the melanistic form of the peppered moth is in retreat. In places such as Manchester, where in 1898 it constituted nearly 100 percent of the moth population, it's now below 5 percent. Natural selection is once again in action!

Galápagos Island finches

Evolution is not only about adapting to changing conditions of life, such as air pollution, or the introduction of dairy farming; it's also about the emergence of new species. Darwin's theory described how this could happen, but he himself had very few examples of the process. The famous Galápagos finches, however, were a fine example—specifically of the phenomenon which evolutionary biologists call "adaptive radiation".

Imagine a territory being colonised by a species newly arrived from elsewhere (as the distant ancestors of the Galápagos finches might have done, had they perhaps been blown over from the mainland in a storm). And imagine "empty niches" available in the ecosystem, such as potential food resources not being utilised by the endemic fauna. In such a case, the newly arrived species might undergo multiple rapid adaptations, "radiating" out to fill the available niches. Species which do this have the advantage of being able to establish themselves in the absence of competition from any already established species in the area.

The Galápagos finches' ancestors presumably arrived in the islands at a time when there were no other (or hardly any) birds present. The first finch to develop a slightly more powerful beak than the others would have an advantage, because it could eat slightly bigger seeds and could have them all to itself. In the same way, the bird which developed a more pointed beak could supplement its diet with insects too hard to catch with a general-purpose beak. Darwin, seeing this pattern, described it in his journals in 1839, long before publishing *On the Origin of Species* but after formulating his theory both in his mind and on paper. "The most curious fact is the perfect gradation in the size of the beaks in the different species of *Geospiza*, from one as large as that of a hawfinch to that of a chaffinch, and ... even to that of a warbler ...", he wrote. "Seeing this gradation and diversity of structure in one small, intimately related group of birds, one might really fancy that from an original paucity of birds in this archipelago, one species had been taken and modified for different ends".[10]

Darwin's delay

Darwin had put all the pieces of the origin of species jigsaw together by the end of the 1830s and soon began to talk about it as "my theory". In the course of 1842, he made what he called a "pencil sketch", 35 pages long, which he wrote up in 1844 as a considerably longer "essay". Darwin clearly recognised that he had made a very significant contribution to the understanding of species and their evolution; for this reason, he now wrote a letter to his wife Emma, to be opened only in the event of his untimely death, in which he asked her to make sure that £400 was set aside for the publication of his theory. "I wish that my sketch be given to some competent person, with this sum to induce him to take trouble in its improvement & enlargement ...".[11] The first man Darwin thought of was Lyell: "Mr Lyell would be the best if he would undertake it: I believe he wd find the work pleasant & he wd learn some facts new to him", he wrote, but "the next best Editor would be Professor Forbes of London". One can almost hear Darwin thinking as he writes, considering first one colleague then another: "The next best (& quite best in many respects) would be Professor Henslow??" And what about Hooker? "Dr Hooker would perhaps correct the Botanical Part, probably—he would do as Editor —Dr Hooker would be very good". Darwin concluded the letter with the instruction that if Emma could not get anyone to take on the editing work, she should just make sure it got published as it stood, not forgetting to point out that it had been written some years previously and had not been intended for publication in its existing form.

Once formulated, Darwin's theory was allowed to lie on the shelf for many years. "Never take down your gun when once up",[12] Darwin wrote once in his private notes on guns and shooting. Perhaps he followed this rule when out shooting, but he certainly didn't apply the same principle to the rest of life. In fact, 15 years would pass since first committing his "sketch" to paper before the wider public heard that one of life's great mysteries had been solved. Such a delay in publication is exceptional in the scientific world and has been much discussed by historians and Darwinologists. Was "Darwin's delay" due to fears of a negative reaction? Was he concerned about offending Emma's religious sentiments? Or was he simply not yet quite finished with the theory?

No doubt Darwin was aware that his ideas were controversial and would challenge many preconceptions shared by laymen and experts alike. Scarcely had he finished his "essay" when he got an emphatic reminder of this. In October 1844, a book titled *Vestiges of the Natural History of Creation* was published anonymously in London. Ranging far and wide in an attempt to unify geology, biology, cosmology, and philosophy, it emphasised the continuous transmutation of all things in the universe and ridiculed the idea of each individual species being created by divine *fiat*. An international bestseller, the book was reprinted in numerous editions and revisions and provoked an enormous amount of discussion.

The clerics were not as happy with the book as the reformers and freethinkers, of course. Some were outraged. To them, taking God out of the processes of natural history meant abolishing all morality and decency. This could lead to a collapse of society, warned the priests and theologians. However, many leading scientists also reacted strongly against the book, for different reasons: Adam Sedgwick, Darwin's former tutor at Cambridge, nevertheless shredded the book in reviewing it, even suggesting that the shaky science it included could only mean it was written by a woman. This was an erroneous assumption, however. As Darwin correctly guessed from the start, the man responsible was Scottish author and publisher Robert Chambers; the secret was successfully concealed from the public until ten years after Chambers's death in 1871.

Both Darwin and his friend and colleague Hooker read *Vestiges* immediately, commenting on it in their letters. Hooker found the book extremely interesting, but Darwin was less enthusiastic. There were too many careless mistakes in the science: "His geology strikes me as bad, & his zoology far worse", he wrote.[13] Maybe Darwin took from the story of *Vestiges* that it was wise to make sure in advance that all one's arguments were bullet-proof, if one were going to take God out of the picture when explaining the evolution of species.

The confession

It was to Hooker that Darwin first confided what he had been thinking, in a letter written in 1844. Darwin sensed that in Hooker he had found a worthy colleague—if not a like-minded person, then at least one he could respect and who respected him. After some chit-chat about the flora of coral atolls and volcanic islands, and the relationship between the number of species and genera on islands, he edged closer to the dangerous subject of whether species could change or whether they were constant. "I have been now ever since my return engaged in a very presumptuous work & which I know no one individual who wd not say a very foolish one", he declared with characteristic cautiousness. "I was so struck with distribution of Galápagos organisms &c &c & with the character of the American fossil mammifers, &c &c that I determined to collect blindly every sort of fact, which cd bear any way on what are species". Before wrenching out his secret, Darwin stressed that he had read widely on both agriculture and horticulture, but then it came: "At last gleams of light have come, & I am almost convinced (quite contrary to opinion I started with) that species are not (it is like confessing a murder) immutable". [14]

The unsayable was said, and Darwin waited with bated breath for Hooker's reaction. Would he cut him dead, or had he found a man he could actually discuss his most heretical ideas with? At first, Hooker was in no hurry to answer, and Darwin even sent him a second letter. Finally he replied, in a sober tone but not at all dismissively. In fact, Hooker's opinion was that entire series of new species had indeed arisen in different places at different times "... and also a gradual change of species", as he wrote to Darwin. "I shall be delighted to hear how you think that this change may have taken place, as no presently conceived opinions satisfy me on the subject", he continued. [15]

This was definitely an opening rather than the rebuttal Darwin feared, and subsequently he began to gradually share his secret with others, although he certainly didn't broadcast the news to the world. One of the next to be confided in was Leonard Jenyns, whom Darwin had brought in to work on the fish specimens from the *Beagle* voyage. Jenyns got the same lead-in as Hooker, from the fauna of the Galápagos and the mammal fossils of South America to Darwin's thorough research on plant selection and animal breeding. "A long searching amongst agricultural & horticultural books & people, makes me believe (I well know how absurdly presumptuous this must appear) that I see the way in which new varieties become exquisitely adapted to the external conditions of life", [16] he wrote to Jenyns.

Jenyns did not dismiss Darwin's acceptance of transmutation, either, although he suggested that there were issues with the word "mutation". In his reply, Darwin assured him that "it will be years before I publish, so that I shall have plenty of time to think of better words".[17] Those words turned out to be far truer than he had realised at the time. The meticulous study of barnacles took him so much more time than anticipated, yet Darwin knew that he was on to something; as time progressed, he became increasingly convinced. "But I can hardly explain what I mean, & you will perhaps wish my Barnacles & Species theory al Diabolo together", he wrote jokingly to Hooker in 1848, "but I don't care what you say, my species theory is all gospel".[18]

CHAPTER 8

Out of the Closet

THE DARWINS LIVED a quiet family life in Downe. Here, Darwin would spend the rest of his days, only rarely travelling anywhere else. It did happen occasionally that he would go up to London to participate in a scientific meeting or to meet colleagues and friends at his club, the Athenaeum, but more often than not he would decline invitations on the grounds of his poor health. On the other hand, he liked to have visitors at Down House, where Owen, Lyell, Hooker, and later Huxley, too, would often come to visit.

At the bottom of the garden, Darwin had a path made, looping for a quarter of a mile or so around a copse and between the meadows. A stroll around the Sand Walk, as it was called, became a part of his daily routine and was where he cogitated on whatever problems he was working on. A particularly tricky question might involve several circuits, and he even used a pile of stones to count how many times he had been round. Even when he didn't feel well, he would usually manage a few turns around the Sand Walk.

The children were educated at home while they were little. Darwin involved them all in his practical studies, getting them to help with making observations and carrying out small experiments.

By the 1850s, he had already had a team of seven little research assistants, but then tragedy struck the family. In 1851, the Darwins' eldest daughter, Annie, died after a difficult illness. This wasn't the first child they had lost; in 1842, little Mary had died when only a few weeks old. But the loss of ten-year-old Annie hit Charles and Emma very hard. Trying desperately to save her, Darwin had brought her to the same doctor at Malvern Spa who, he thought, had helped him with a water cure when he was at his worst. Like her father, the poor child was also wrapped in cold, wet sheets; but fortunately, after a while both Darwin and the doctor saw that it wasn't helping and concentrated instead on reducing her suffering as she weakened. Emma, heavily pregnant at the time, had to stay home in Kent. Charles kept his wife updated with daily letters telling of the small improvements in their daughter's condition—and of the many setbacks.

"Our poor child has been fearfully ill; as ill as a human being could be: it was dreadful that night the Dr. told me it would probably be all over before morning".[1] When Annie finally died, it fell to a heartbroken Darwin to tell Emma and the rest of the family what had happened. "She was my favourite child; her cordiality, openness, buoyant joyousness & strong affection made her most loveable",[2] he wrote to his cousin William Fox. A few weeks later, Emma was safely delivered of a fifth son, Horace, but the death of Annie remained a devastating loss for the Darwins.

Assembling the evidence

After completing his "essay" on the origin of species, Darwin focused on collecting more information to support his theory. Something which interested him very much was the way in which farmers and growers could modify species as they sought to improve their strains of domesticated animals and cultivated plants. In fact, he saw clear parallels between natural selection and the artificial selection undertaken by breeders and horticulturists. He gathered information on the entire subject by means of an extensive written correspondence with anyone he could find who might know something about raising domesticated animals or plant propagation.

"Do not forget to make enquiries about origin, even if only traditionally known, of any vars. of domestic quadrupeds, birds, silkworms &c.", Darwin wrote to Hooker when he was on an expedition to India, adding a request for a hive of domestic bees if he should come across one.[3] To his cousin, William Fox, he wrote requesting any purebred poultry he had to spare: "I wd beg a chicken with exact age stated about a week or fortnight old! to be sent in Box by Post. Indeed I shd be very glad to have a nestling common pigeon sent, for I mean to make skeletons, & have already just begun comparing wild & tame ducks".[4] He had no need of a mastiff, and he already had bulldog and greyhound puppies preserved in salt, but if one of Fox's turkeys should die, Darwin would be very glad to have it sent on to him. And if Fox's half-bred African cat should happen to die, he must send the corpse so that Darwin could get the skeleton. "Perhaps all this will only bother you — So I will add no more", he wrote considerately. Nevertheless, he immediately continued: "Should you ever have opportunity when in Derbyshire, do enquire for me, from some person you told me of whether offspring of male muscovy & female common duck, resembles offspring of female muscovy & male common".[5]

The garden at Down House began to resemble a menagerie. Darwin decided to breed pigeons himself, in order to get a better understanding of the different races. He was convinced that, however strange pigeon-fanciers' breeds had become—with spectacular white fan-tails or crests on their heads—they were all derived from the same wild rock doves. When Darwin finally began to write his *magnum opus* on the origin of species, the first chapter was all about pigeon breeding. Studying the breeding of domestic animals, and especially the artificial breeding of prettified versions of wild original species, could hardly be considered science at all for most scientists of the day, but for Darwin it illustrated an important point. If, from ordinary rock doves, selective breeding could produce fantails, frills, and pouters in such a short time, then just imagine what natural selection might accomplish, given millions of years.

Lyell's good advice

Darwin's circle of scientist friends and colleagues expanded at the beginning of the 1850s to include Thomas Huxley, who was in many ways the opposite of Darwin. From a modest background, he was largely self-taught as a result of his own efforts. Obliged to leave school at the age of ten due to his family's financial difficulties, he nevertheless showed exceptional intellectual gifts, teaching himself to read German, Latin, and Greek as well as study geology and the natural sciences. Scholarships to study anatomy and medicine followed, until he joined the Royal Navy with a position as assistant surgeon, which allowed him to pursue his interest in natural history, like many other medical men of the time. Also like them, he set off in 1846 at the age of 21 on his first voyage, an expedition to New Guinea and Australia. There he lost no time in collecting specimens, writing up his observations, and sending articles home to be published in England. By the time Darwin got to know him, he had made numerous important discoveries in the field of marine invertebrates and was a rising star in the scientific world, as recognised by his election to the Royal Society and the award of the Royal Society Medal at the tender age of 26.

Over dinner at Down House in the spring of 1856, attended by Hooker and Huxley—now a professor—among others, Darwin aired his thoughts about species and their evolution. Shortly afterwards, he also shared the same ideas with Lyell. For Lyell, this was something of a bombshell; his own ideas could probably admit the idea of Earth undergoing changes, but certainly not species. Still, after recovering somewhat, he hastened to encourage Darwin to publish his theories. If he didn't, someone else would perhaps have the same ideas and publish first, thus winning all the credit. "I wish you would publish some small fragment of your data — pigeons if you please — & so out with the theory & let it take date — & be cited — & understood", urged Lyell.[6] This sound advice left Darwin in two minds. "With respect to your suggestion of a sketch of my view; I hardly know what to think, but will reflect on it", he replied. "I rather hate the idea of writing for priority, yet I certainly shd be vexed if any one were to publish my doctrines before me".[7] Then as now, priority was everything in the scientific world. Thus goaded, Darwin at long last began to write. But it was already too late.

A letter from Wallace

Lyell's concern that someone else would pre-empt Darwin was not without foundation. An indication that others were indeed interested in the same subject was offered in 1855, when Darwin read an article by Alfred Wallace, then working in Borneo, on the distribution of animals and plants on the island of Sarawak. Wallace was getting alarmingly close to Darwin's territory when he formulated what would come to be known as his Sarawak Law: "Every species has come into existence coincident both in space and time with a closely allied species".[8] Darwin somehow didn't see the threat, or didn't take it seriously. However, he did write a friendly letter to Wallace, gently pointing out that he himself was also working with these problems, had in fact been busy with them for 20 years, and was now preparing his observations and thoughts for publication.[9]

If this was supposed to be a warning flag advising Wallace that this field of research was "occupied", then one must conclude that Wallace didn't get the hint. In June 1858, another letter from Wallace landed in Darwin's mailbox. Still over on the other side of the world, in Malaysia now, he had come to the same conclusions as Darwin and by more or less the same reasoning. Like Darwin, he had fastened onto the way species varied and had looked closely at the biogeographical distribution of animals and plants, both on a local scale and a continental scale. Like Darwin, he had also read Malthus. During a period of fever, while he was forced to spend many hours a day lying down, everything fell into place. Species evolved, and this happened because nature constantly eliminated the least fit individuals. He called the mechanism "natural selection", just as Darwin did, and formulated his thoughts in an article which he sent to—of all people—Darwin.

In his letter, Wallace also asked Darwin to show the enclosed article to Lyell, the big gun in the scientific world. Lyell was the ideal man to turn to, but Wallace had never met him. Darwin, on the other hand, knew Lyell personally, so it was natural to ask for an introduction in that way.

Deeply shaken, Darwin read the letter and the article. Here was his own theory, almost word for word. In dismay, he took up his pen to Lyell: "Your words have come true with a vengeance that I shd be forestalled. . . . I never saw a more striking coincidence. If Wallace had my M.S. sketch written out in 1842 he could not have made a better short abstract! Even his terms now stand as Heads of my Chapters", he wrote. Although Wallace had not asked Darwin to forward the article to a journal for publication—but only to show it to Lyell—Darwin nevertheless offered to do just that, if Lyell thought it were the proper thing to do, while at the same time bemoaning his misfortune: "So all my originality, whatever it may amount to, will be smashed".[10]

Hooker was soon drawn into the discussion, and letters flew back and forth among the three men. Darwin was caught in an uncomfortable moral dilemma. On the one hand, as a gentleman he could hardly send his own manuscript for publication now, knowing that Wallace had formulated the same ideas; what's more Wallace had entrusted his own paper to Darwin to decide how to proceed with it. On the other hand, Darwin could hardly bear to think that all he had worked for so intensively for over 20 years should now come to nothing. "But as I had not intended to publish any sketch, can I do so honourably (just) because Wallace has sent me an outline of his doctrine?— I would far rather burn my whole book than that he or any man shd think that I had behaved in a paltry spirit. Do you not think his having sent me this sketch ties my hands?"[11] Darwin asked Lyell a week later.

Joint presentation to the Linnean Society

As if this weren't enough, the village of Downe was hit by scarlet fever, and many of the inhabitants were seriously ill. The Darwins' youngest child was one of those whose life hung in the balance, so at this anxious time Darwin left it to Lyell and Hooker to handle the matter. An opportunity arose for them to engineer a clever solution when the Linnean Society called an extraordinary general meeting on July 1 to elect a new member. Like two musketeers, Hooker and Lyell stepped into the breach to ensure that Wallace's and Darwin's theories would be presented at the meeting in a way that acknowledged both men's contributions to science. To ensure that posterity would understand and recognise what they both saw as Darwin's priority, extracts were read both from his 1844 essay and from an 1857 letter to his American colleague Asa Gray at Harvard University, in which he had included a synopsis of his theory. Finally, Wallace's article, "An

Essay on the Tendency of Varieties, &c. to depart indefinitely from the Original Type", was read aloud.

Darwin was not present at this historic occasion. His son had died three days previously, and the burial took place July 1. He could hardly think of anything but his family at this time. Wallace was not there, either, of course: he was still in Malaysia. In fact, no one even asked him whether he approved of the way in which his appeal to Darwin ended up being handled. A lesser man might have been peeved at not being asked about sharing the honours with another. Not Wallace, however. As he recalled later, "Of course I not only approved, but felt that they had given me more honour and credit than I deserved, by putting my sudden intuition—hastily written and immediately sent off for the opinion of Darwin and Lyell—on the same level with the prolonged labours of Darwin, who had reached the same point twenty years before me".[12]

One cannot say that the presentation which we regard today as one of the defining moments in the history of the natural sciences was actually seen as such at the time. Nor can one even say that anyone actually took any notice at all! On the contrary, the president of the Linnean Society, Thomas Bell, concluded in his annual review that "The year which has passed has not, indeed, been marked by any of those striking discoveries which at once revolutionize, so to speak, the department of science on which they bear".[13]

Sexual selection

Darwin and Wallace had thought along very similar lines, but on one point they disagreed. Darwin believed that natural selection included a phenomenon which he called sexual selection. Wallace disagreed, but most of the discussion on this issue occurred after Darwin's death and thus without his involvement. Today, most biologists agree with

Darwin that sexual selection is an important part of the mechanism of evolution.

An obvious difference between males and females of the same species is that they have different sex organs. But, as Darwin and many others before him pointed out, there are often many other differences which make it easy to tell a male from a female. Elephant seal bulls are more than twice the size of the cows and have a strange, trunk-like proboscis—from which they get their name. The male narwhal boasts a long, straight tusk; the bull elk carries a rack of antlers; and in many bird species, the breeding males are resplendent with colourful plumage. Even with species where the sexes look similar, their behaviour can be very different. The male bowerbird spends days decorating his bower with colourful flowers and leaves, the humpback whale sings long and complex songs for his potential mates, and male frogs can croak all night.

Darwin saw that it was a tough challenge to explain a peacock's enormous tail feathers, an elk's heavy antlers, or a rhinoceros beetle's strange horn as something created by means of "normal" selective processes. After all, how would it benefit an individual to carry a huge tail or a heavy set of antlers around all the time? Such features were more of a nuisance and a disadvantage in the struggle for survival, Darwin argued, "unless the individual who carried it thereby gained some other advantage, for example by being more attractive to potential mates and by passing this advantage on to the next generation".[14]

So if both the male's tendency to grow a fine set of antlers or a spectacular tail, and the females' tendency to prefer males with large antlers and long tails, are hereditary, then we have a mechanism which will drive the evolution of a species in that direction, even if it confers no other advantages. This is the mechanism Darwin called "sexual selection".

Darwin used the rhinoceros beetle as one example of sexual selection. Many different species of rhinoceros beetles have developed fantastic "antlers" or "horns". Their ancestors are thought to have lived in burrows, where it was no doubt an advantage to be able to defend a burrow against other beetles. This explains why the ability to grow horns is so widespread in the family; they would be useful in defending territory. Once horns are present, sexual selection can incentivise the development of the almost grotesque horns which we see in the beetles today.

The classical demonstration of sexual selection, males fighting for possession of females, is seen in many different species. For example, elephant seals fight for access to breeding females; because the females are hauled out on a beach at the time, this includes maintaining a territory free of other males. Such behaviour naturally favours the biggest and strongest individual males. An alpha male seal, known as a "beach master", can in this way guard a harem of up to 100 females. This requires him to be a giant, weighing more than 2.5 tonnes—nearly four times the weight of the females. And he must be serious about his exclusion zone on the beach: anything that moves in his area gets attacked, including sea lions or any human beings (such as researchers) who happen to be on the beach!

For a male who doesn't have a territory or a harem to defend, there is little to lose by starting a fight: if he doesn't, he will lose out in the reproduction game. So the beach at mating time resembles a battlefield, with constant bloody clashes and confrontations. However, a small number of males usually find a way to avoid the fighting and still gain access to females. Keeping a very low profile around the perimeter of the territory, where the risk of drawing the beach master's attention is lowest, they sneak in when he is busy beating someone else up.[15] This strategy is sufficiently successful that at least a few males try it in every population of elephant seals.

Female choice

Darwin also noticed that not only male size and fighting ability determined who gained access to females for mating. The females also had a not insignificant say in the matter. "The female … with the rarest exception, is less eager than the male", he wrote. "The female, though comparatively passive, generally exerts some choice and accepts one male in preference to others. The exertion of some choice on the part of the female seems almost as general a law as the eagerness of the male".[16]

With a number of bird species, female choice is seen very clearly. In the breeding season, both ruff and black grouse perform a ritual courtship dance—the lek—at specific places known as lekking grounds. Several males may each occupy a patch of territory on the same "dance floor". The females congregate nearby, apparently choosing males to mate with according to their performance in the dance. For most of the year, the male ruff looks to the untrained eye like any other medium-sized brownish wader; but in the breeding season, he develops the spectacular collar of raised feathers from which he gets his name. The males occupying the centre of the arena have black or dark-coloured collars, while those lingering around the edges have white or pale-coloured collars. The dark-coloured males are territorial and try to entice the females to their own spot on the dance floor. The pale-coloured males don't control any territory, but they try to gain access to the females by hanging around the edges and jumping in whenever they get the chance. A third group of ruffs has a strategy similar to that of the low-profile elephant seals: their plumage mimics the females' plumage exactly, so they can sneakily find mating opportunities by mixing with the crowd of admiring females around the dance arena.[17]

With marine iguanas (which Darwin encountered close up during his *Beagle* voyage), the males also occupy territory to which they try to attract females. A male without a territory has little chance with the females—which could explain why the iguana tossed so carelessly by Darwin into the sea was so anxious to return to the same spot each time he regained the land.

Even the everyday phenomenon of birdsong has a double function: males sing not just to announce to other males that they are occupying a territory, but also to give females the chance to choose the singer they prefer. With both "dancing" and singing birds, as well as any other animal which "performs", one can imagine that performance qualities can provide information on how strong and "fit" for survival the male is. Such qualities can be passed on to offspring, so perhaps the female should take note of them in selecting a mate.

Another example, the humpback whale, sings a very long and complicated underwater song that can be heard at a great distance. It has been suggested that this song tells any females in the area something about the male's fitness. In any case, it shows that he can hold his breath underwater for a long time. Presumably, the bigger and stronger the animal, the longer he can hold his breath and thus continue to sing.[18]

The handicapped male

There is an apparent paradox in the need for males to win the favours of females by equipping themselves with massive antlers, long tails, bright colours, and enormous tusks. A peacock with a tail the size of a bridal train is a sitting target for predators and cannot easily escape. Brightly coloured birds or frogs are much more conspicuous to their enemies than green or brown ones, which can hide in the undergrowth; huge, clumsy antlers make it hard for a deer to move around under trees and bushes. This led Israeli biologist Amotz Zahavi to suggest that the development of such attributes signals that the male in question is "fit for fight" despite the handicap he is carrying around.[19] Thus the peacock with a splendid spread of tail feathers is, in effect, announcing that he's so good at escaping predators, feeding himself, and staying healthy and parasite-free that he can afford to develop such a spectacularly useless accessory as his impressive tail.

Conflict between the sexes

The theory of sexual selection has been developed in several new directions since Darwin laid aside his fountain pen. One very significant addition came in the 1970s, when American biologist Rob Trivers expanded it with an analysis of the conflict which, he claimed, exists between the sexes.[20] This starts already with the gametes or sex cells. Because a typical egg is many thousands of times bigger than a sperm, the female must invest more energy to produce an egg than a male does to produce a sperm cell. In nearly all animals, the female's investment in the fertilised egg is also much more significant than the male's. In mammals, the foetus develops inside the female's body, draining her resources massively for weeks and months; this period is followed by further costly nurturing in the form of supplying milk and generally taking care of the infant for a considerable time after birth.

According to Trivers, this imbalance means that the interests of males and females are different. If we assume that they both have the same goal—namely, to produce the maximum number of surviving offspring—then the female will achieve this best by being very careful who she mates with. Since each egg, and each conception, represents such a significant investment, the female will very carefully choose the best possible partner she can. The male, on the other hand, has little to lose. A sperm cell here or there doesn't matter, as they are so tiny and demand such a small investment. Thus it is in his interests to mate with as many females as possible in order to maximise the chances of passing on his genes. Of course, there are many exceptions to this rule; for example, with many bird species (and also some mammals), the survival of their young depends on both parents helping to raise them.

CHAPTER 9

The masterpiece

AFTER THE PRESENTATION at the Linnean Society, Darwin was busier than ever. His reputation now rested on whether he could live up to the claims he had made: that the major book he had been working on for years was nearly ready and that the extracts which had been read aloud were just a sample of his thinking, with much more to come. Now it was time to finish the job.

Darwin had originally planned to produce a comprehensive and exhaustive work as his contribution to science, but now he found himself compelled by circumstances to compress it into what he called "an abstract of my work". He laboured intensively over it, and the "abstract" steadily grew. In March 1859, Darwin wrote to Lyell, asking for advice about how much to tell Murray about the contents: "Would you advise me to tell Murray that my Book is not more un-orthodox, than the subject makes inevitable — That I do not discuss origin of man — That I do not bring in any discussions about Genesis &c, & only give facts, & such conclusions from them, as seem to me fair?" he asked. "Or had I better say nothing to Murray, & assume that he cannot object to this much unorthodoxy, which in fact is not more than any Geological Treatise, which runs slap counter to Genesis? Darwin concluded by asking what Lyell thought of his proposed title[1]:

An abstract of an Essay
on the
Origin
of
Species and Varieties
Through Natural Selection

We don't know what Lyell thought, but Murray was not impressed. "An abstract of an essay!" one can almost hear him say, "that will never do; I have to sell this book, after all". Darwin wriggled and resisted, but Murray did manage to axe those words—even though the final solution used on the title page still sounds to our ears rather long and laboured: "*On the Origin of Species by means of Natural Selection, or the preservation of favoured races in the struggle for life*".

At over 500 pages when it finally came out in November 1859, the book could hardly be called an abstract—or even an essay—any more, though Darwin still insisted this was only the short version of what he called "his theory". As the publication date drew near, Darwin was busy sending out as many as 80 advance copies to friends, colleagues, and reviewers. He wrote in particular to some of those who, he thought, would react the most violently to his work—in an attempt to draw the sting of their likely resistance. One such was Richard Owen, to whom he wrote: "I fear that it will be abominable in your eyes; but I assure you that it is the result of far more labour than is apparent on its face".[2] For Hugh Falconer, a member of the Royal Society and one of the great English natural historians, a slightly more humorous tone was appropriate: "Lord, how savage you will be, if you read it, and how you will long to crucify me alive! I fear it will produce no other effect on you; but if it should stagger you in ever so slight a degree, in this case, I am fully convinced that you will become, year after year, less fixed in your belief in the immutability of species[3]." Henslow and Sedgwick, his old Cambridge tutors, each received a copy, with the assurance that the book contained no expression of disrespect to them.

Darwin's sense that his book could be controversial was not mistaken. In contrast to the lukewarm reception which the Linnean Society had given his ideas, the release of *On the Origin of Species* to the general public was an immediate success. Today we would almost call it a bestseller. The first edition, sold in advance of publication, created an immediate buzz, so a second, larger run was promptly ordered. One aspect of the book's success was without a doubt its accessibility to non-specialists. It rarely happens that one person, with one stroke, changes our understanding of how the world is put together but even more rarely does he express himself in such a way that any educated person can follow his reasoning.

Darwin himself was somewhat surprised by the book's success. Although he had indeed intended it for the general public rather than just scientists, he was still taken aback to hear how widespread was the demand. In January 1860, Emma received a letter from an acquaintance who had overheard a man asking for the book at a kiosk at Waterloo Bridge railway station. It was, unfortunately, sold out, but the kiosk owner stated he had heard it was a remarkable book.

Content of *On the Origin of Species*

On the Origin of Species is a long book, and Darwin used numerous examples from all over the world and from both plant and animal kingdoms to illustrate his points. Turkeys and turnips, laurels and lions, rattlesnakes and racehorses, orchids and ostriches—nothing was too big or too small to win a place in this book. He presents his thesis judiciously, like a lawyer in court carefully building a case bit by bit from a detailed collection of evidence.

In *On the Origin of Species*, Darwin concluded that evolution had taken place. The Earth is not a place where everything is unchanging and constant; on the contrary, it is a place of incessant change. It certainly wasn't created recently, either. The strongest body of evidence to that effect came from geology: in the oldest layers, there were organisms which simply no longer existed, while some forms (such as the mammals) clearly arose relatively recently.

Darwin also argued that all organisms on Earth were descended from a common ancestor. When we say that finches belong to a group of related birds, it means they are related to each other. Similarly, if the extinct giant sloths had features in common with sloths living today, it was because they had at one point had a common ancestor. It was this part of Darwin's reasoning which got people talking, for even if Darwin himself very carefully avoided saying so, the human species implicitly must also have common ancestors with other animals. Even if being an anatomist (like Owen) certainly helped, specialist knowledge wasn't necessary to figure out in which animal family to look to find ancestors to the human species.

Darwin concluded that new species can arise when established species develop in different directions. He had seen evidence for this both on the Galápagos and under the microscope, when he was engaged in his long study of barnacles. The Galápagos finches had perhaps been important for Darwin's understanding of the evolution of species, but in his *magnum opus* they received just a mention in passing. Much more central to the book was the mechanism to which he attributed the evolution of new species—namely, natural selection. Invoking the analogy of the selection processes used by plant and animal breeders, he presented the reader with principles he believed also functioned in nature. Here, it was simply the struggle for survival which would sort the well fitted from the less fitted. "It may be said that natural selection is daily and hourly scrutinising, throughout the world, every variation, even the slightest; rejecting that which is bad, preserving and adding up all that is good",[4] as he wrote in the book's fourth chapter.

Darwin also explained at length how the variations he saw within species led to the creation of new species, gradually and over long periods of time. Lyell's exposition of the extensive reach of geological time had not been lost on Darwin, and the gradual development of new species over similar aeons was becoming clearer as fossil evidence accumulated. This development also found a parallel in the processes which were seen in plant and animal breeding. New breeds of horses or dogs didn't appear from one day to the next, either. Darwin concluded the book with a powerful and poetic appreciation of the new world view he presented: "There is grandeur in this view of life, with its several powers, having been originally breathed into a few forms or into one; and that, whilst this planet has gone cycling on according to the fixed law of gravity, from so simple a beginning endless forms most beautiful and most wonderful have been, and are being, evolved".[5]

The book's reception

That the book was relatively easy to read, even without any prior knowledge of the subject, meant that many readers were also able to get involved in the debates that followed its publication. In his characteristic manner, Darwin made himself more or less invisible and let others fight his battles for him. There was no shortage of contenders. Huxley stepped forward to review the book in favourable terms; Hooker was also positive, of course; and Asa Gray, Darwin's friend and colleague at Harvard, was responsible for a glowing review in the American press.

Not all reactions and reviews were positive, however. The critical voices fell into two camps: those concerned that Darwin was undermining the world view of the Bible and of the church (this was hard to dispute), and those who pointed to weaknesses in the arguments from a more scientific viewpoint. Chief among the latter was Richard Owen, who was to become one of Darwin's most dogged critics. They met shortly after the book's publication, but it was an uncomfortable meeting. Under a veneer of politeness, Owen's hostility and arrogance were barely concealed: he struggled to find anything complimentary to say to his former good friend. "We do not want to know what Darwin believes & is convinced of, but what he can prove",[6] Owen sneered. Darwin willingly acknowledged the point and admitted that his work was lacking in that area. He even promised to try to modify some of the "I believe" and "I am convinced" statements in a future edition. But Owen only rubbed salt in the wounds: "You will then spoil your book, the charm of it is that it is Darwin himself".[7]

Owen also authored a particularly churlish and dismissive review of *On the Origin of Species* which appeared anonymously in the *Edinburgh Review* in 1860. Owen's authorship was readily revealed by the frequent favourable references to his own opinions and publications. What once had been a friendship based on mutual respect and admiration (and, no doubt, also on the fact that each had use for the other in furthering their own careers) became, as the years went by, a bitter and irreconcilable enmity. When Owen later became involved in a more heated controversy with Hooker, Darwin naturally supported Hooker and wrote to him about Owen: "I used to be ashamed of hating him so much, but now I will carefully cherish my hatred & contempt to the last day of my life."[8]

Problems with the theory

The big hole in the evidence for Darwin's theory was the lack of transitional forms in the fossil record. Although Darwin had tried to counter the objections he expected to receive from critics by devoting an entire chapter to this subject, he did not succeed. This was exactly where his most serious opponents attacked him. If all species had evolved gradually from others, why could we not find these "missing links" as fossils? To such questions, Darwin could only reiterate what he had already written in *On Origin of Species*: "I can answer these questions and grave objections only on the supposition that the geological record is far more imperfect than most geologists believe."[9]

Darwin correctly understood that the great majority of animals and plants leave no traces behind after they die. They are either eaten by other animals, or, most likely, they just decompose slowly. Bones are the last parts to disappear, but with the help of sun and wind and rain and frost, they also crumble to dust. For a plant or animal to become fossilised, on the other hand, it must be covered with sand or mud sediment immediately after death in order to protect it from the effects of weather or disturbance by scavengers. Then many further layers of sediment must cover it, in order to begin the fossilisation process. However, if the dead animal or plant lies in a forest, on a mountainside, or on any other upland site, this will never happen. The only possibility to cover a specimen in layers of sediment is if it comes to rest in a riverbed or lakebed, or in the sea. Soft tissues normally decompose rapidly, leaving only bones and structural fibres behind. Then, over a period of millions of years, a gradual change takes place: waterborne minerals from surrounding sediments slowly replace the minerals of the original tissues. Following the ensuing geological processes of compaction and pressurisation, the organism becomes petrified or fossilised.

Of the few specimens which undergo this long sequence of processes, the majority are never found, because they lie deeply buried in sedimentary layers underneath the ocean floors or riverbeds. For a fossil to be found and recovered, the layer in which it is embedded must somehow be exposed, whether through geological upheavals and subsequent erosion or in the course of mining and quarrying activities. Fewer plant than animal fossils can be used as evidence of evolution—not because plants are less evolved but because they leave even fewer fossils behind than animals do. Plants obviously lack bones, and they seldom contain much in the way of hard shells and other structures which can become fossilised.

In Darwin's day, palaeontology was a new science; very few fossils had been properly classified. Darwin knew that the chances of a fossil being formed in the first place *and* of its being found later were infinitesimal. No doubt he would have been delighted to know that future generations of palaeontologists would find plenty of fossils to confirm his theories.

Archaeopteryx is found

The first "missing link" was actually found while Darwin was still alive. In a limestone quarry at Solnhofen in what is now southern Germany, an unusually fine and well-preserved fossil turned up. It was unmistakably a birdlike creature, with wings and feathers; but unlike birds, it had teeth, a long and bony tail, and claws on both feet and wings.

To the great regret of the Germans, the first specimen of *Archaeopteryx* found ended up in London. It was sold for £700—at that time a princely sum—to the British Museum, where Richard Owen waited eagerly to receive it. Shortly afterwards, an even finer and even better preserved *Archaeopteryx* specimen turned up at Solnhofen, and this time it stayed in Germany. It can still be viewed at the Natural History Museum of Berlin and is naturally regarded as one of their greatest treasures.

The London *Archaeopteryx* was nearly as good a specimen, and many of the inner circle of contemporary scientists paid visits to the museum to admire this exciting new fossil. Hugh Falconer, himself a pioneering palaeontologist as well as a natural historian, wrote delightedly to Darwin: "Had the Solnhofen quarries been commissioned—by august command—to turn out a strange being à la Darwin—it could not have executed the behest more handsomely—than in the Archæopteryx".[10] Owen had wasted no time in preparing his description of the new fossil and presenting it to the Royal Society. But Darwin shouldn't pay too much attention to "the slip-shod and hasty account" given by Owen, said Falconer. "It is a much more astounding creature than has entered into the conception of the describer", he asserted. Owen, determined not to give any credence to Darwin's theory, saw no transitional features in *Archaeopteryx*: it was a bird, admittedly a strange one, with teeth and a bony tail, but definitely still a bird, as he explained to the audience at the Royal Society.

Huxley, seizing the opportunity both to tread on Owen's toes and to support Darwin, stepped up with a new interpretation. He admitted that reptiles and birds were superficially very dissimilar: "To superficial observation no two groups of beings can appear to be more entirely dissimilar than reptiles and birds. Placed side by side, a humming-bird and a tortoise, an ostrich and a crocodile, offer the strongest contrast, and a stork seems to have little but animality in common with the snake it swallows".[11] But he then went on to point out several traits of *Archaeopteryx* which suggested its origins within the reptilian order: the teeth, the long and bony tail, and the claws on the wings. In an article published shortly afterwards, he took the final step of suggesting directly that the birds were descended from dinosaurs.

The debate about the origins of the birds did not stop there, however. In fact, it raged on for more than a hundred years after the deaths of Darwin, Owen, and Huxley. Only in the 1990s were the fossilised remains of feathered dinosaurs first excavated in China, thus confirming that birds did indeed descend from dinosaurs. In fact, one could even say that birds are the only surviving dinosaurs.

Dinosaurs with feathers

Proof that birds are dinosaurs with feathers turned up in Liaoning province in north-eastern China, where amazing finds of fossils have been made in the past 25 years. Fossils from this source are especially revealing, given that the animals were covered in layers of volcanic ash which preserved fine details and even soft tissues. The many species found include crickets with long feelers as well as dragonflies with even the wing veins still visible. But the most extraordinary fossils are of feathered dinosaurs. So far, more than 20 quite distinct species have been found, so clearly feathers were a widespread feature of this region's dinosaurs. Even close relatives of *Tyrannosaurus rex*, the archetypal dinosaur, have been discovered with feathers.

It seems clear that many of the Liaoning dinosaurs couldn't fly, which adds weight to the idea that feathers were originally developed for reasons other than flight. Perhaps their original function was to keep the dinosaurs warm? Insulation is clearly an important property of feathers for most birds, including flightless ones. We also take advantage of their insulating value in the form of down jackets and duvets. Another possibility is that feathers evolved as a way of signalling or communicating between individuals or between species. This function of feathers is still important for birds today.

Four-legged fish

Feathered dinosaur fossils are not the only evidence supporting the theory of evolution. More fossils than Darwin could have dreamt of have now turned up, making links between the different animal groups and, to a lesser extent, the plant groups. In 1899, a location rich in exciting fossils was discovered in eastern Greenland. The Swedish expedition responsible for the find had been on an entirely different mission—a search for any signs of a hot-air-balloon expedition to the North Pole undertaken two years previously by the explorer Salomon Andrée. Members of the expedition had disappeared without trace, but the search party found instead an exciting source of fossils. In 1931, a combined Danish-Swedish expedition was mounted to investigate this desolate coastal area further. They found one of the world's most important fossils ever: the petrified remains of the animal which later would be christened *Ichthyostega*. Thus, one thing can lead to another, and coincidences can be significant even in the scientific world.

Ichthyostega was particularly special because it was the first fossil to link fishes with four-legged animals. Those suggesting that tetrapods—mammals, reptiles, and amphibians—had evolved from fish did not have much to go on except that no other possibilities were available. But *Ichthyostega* suddenly provided that vital missing link between fish and amphibians. Nearly five feet long, *Ichthyostega* had short legs, a long and fishlike tail, and a broad, flattened head—something like a giant salamander. Other tetrapod fossils soon turned up; a second species of "four-legged fish", also found in Greenland, was named *Acanthostega*.

Jenny Clack, Cambridge Professor of Vertebrate Palaeontology, has studied these distant ancestors of all four-legged animals perhaps more than anyone else. Her breakthrough discoveries came after a 1987 expedition to the highlands of north-eastern Greenland, where she collected a number of fossil remains of both *Acanthostega* and

Ichthyostega. Back in the laboratory, she carefully prepared the fossils, which revealed a great surprise. *Acanthostega's* paddle-shaped feet consisted of not five, but rather eight "fingers"—while *Ichthyostega* boasted seven digits. Thus the five-fingered pattern, which all current mammals, amphibians, and reptiles share, was not the original (nor the only) one to evolve.

The two types of tetrapods seem to have enjoyed very different lifestyles. Jenny Clack concluded that *Acanthostega* spent most of its time in the water, crawling around slowly looking for food, while *Ichthyostega* was a much more active and aggressive beast, able to climb out onto land and to move around in both environments.[12] Fossilised trackways made by early tetrapods have been found in several different parts of the world, such as on Valentia Island in County Kerry, Ireland.

The series of finds was made complete when another fossil turned up in 2006, this time on Ellesmere Island, Canada. It was exactly the fossil a palaeontologist would hope to find in looking for a species to fill the gap between *Acanthostega* and *Ichthyostega* and the fishes. *Tiktaalik*—clearly still a fish—has many characteristics of a tetrapod, and its flattened head looks well adapted for life in shallow water. Its pectoral fins have strong bones, suggesting they could at least partly support its body weight. It has lost the bony gill covers which fish have, so its head is free to turn at the neck. Although it still has fin rays, they are smaller than on normal fish. Writing with her colleague Per Ahlberg, Clack compares the importance of *Tiktaalik* to that of *Archaeopteryx*: "It is a link between fishes and land vertebrates that might in time become as much of an evolutionary icon as the proto-bird *Archaeopteryx*".[13]

Jenny Clack proposes that the limb-like fins of *Tiktaalik*, and later the legs of *Acanthostegas* and *Ichthyostegas*, were advantageous for animals living in shallow water over a soft or muddy bottom. Legs did not evolve so that animals could walk on land, but instead so they could get around in shallow water. Only after legs had arisen in water did the evolution of land animals begin to take off.

It has long been known that the place to look for the ancestors of the tetrapods was amongst the lobe-finned fishes. This group differs from other fish in that their fleshy, lobe-shaped fins are attached to their bodies with small bones. Their pectoral and pelvic fins later evolved into the limbs of the tetrapods, and the fin bones became the bones of the fore legs and hind legs. Lobe-finned fish survive to this day as coelacanths and three families of lungfish, but these are not the ancestors of the first tetrapod amphibians. That role has now been attributed to an extinct fish with the name *Elpistostege,* which has many traits in common with *Tiktaalik:* a flattened head with the eyes on top, a bony tail, and some particular bones in the skull not found in other fishes.

It is important to emphasise that *Tiktaalik* is not the ancestor of the quadrupeds, any more than *Archaeopteryx* is the ancestor of the birds. Even so, the existence of these fossils is no less crucial, because they show that transitional forms among different groups of animals did exist.

Whales

Another large group of animals whose origins have been determined by means of the discoveries of more and more fossils is the cetaceans. A very special order of animals, cetaceans diverge in many ways from other mammals. They have no hair or fur, their nasal passages end not at the front of the head in nostrils but on top, in the blowholes. Their hind legs have disappeared, and their front legs have become flippers. And yet they are mammals, giving birth to live young and suckling them. Mammals evolved on land

and were originally adapted to life on land; therefore, whales must have evolved from land-living mammals. Three groups of mammals have "returned to the sea" and adapted to life in a very different life element: seals, sea cows (manatees), and cetaceans. Although these animals have all come to resemble each other in some ways, their origins are quite different.

If Darwin's theory—that species evolved by means of a gradual process over many years—is true, then an entire series of species must have existed in which the gradual development of some of the adaptations seen in cetaceans today can be seen. And that is precisely the story told by the fossil record.

The oldest known fossil cetacean was excavated in Pakistan— hence the very appropriate name *Pakicetus*. It doesn't resemble any whales known today. *Pakicetus*, a small, long-legged predator about the size of a wolf, probably spent much its lifetime chasing fish in shallow seas, lakes, or rivers; but it could also run around and hunt on land. What places it as an ancestor of the cetacean line is the particular bone structure of its inner ear, a feature found in all living and extinct cetaceans but not in other mammals.

Ambulocetus is another fossilised early cetacean from the mountains of Pakistan. From younger geological layers than *Pakicetus*, it shows further adaptations to an aquatic lifestyle: shorter back legs well suited to swimming and—most likely—webbed feet, even though these are not visible in the fossils. *Ambulocetus* probably lived somewhat like today's crocodiles, lurking in shallow water to ambush its prey.

Rhodocetus, also from Pakistan, was somewhat more recent than *Ambulocetus* and even better adapted to life in the water. The hind legs are smaller still, and the nostrils have migrated further from the snout up onto the head. *Rhodocetus* has very short cervical vertebrae, an adaptation seen in all modern cetaceans that prevents the head from bending at the neck. This characteristic seems awkward but is actually very sensible if you want to swim fast. Longer spinous processes on the vertebrae of the backbone also suggest that *Rhodocetus* had strong back muscles—like modern whales, which use these to power a tail fluke up and down in order to drive propulsion. So it is possible that *Rhodocetus* also had a tail fluke.

With *Basilosaurus*, the transformation to a proper whale was nearly complete. *Basilosaurus* fossils have been found in many places round the world; it was first thought to be a large reptile, an aquatic relative of the dinosaurs. None other than Richard Owen showed that *Basilosaurus* was, in fact, not a reptile but a mammal—although he didn't identify it as a whale. Yet it definitely was a whale, and a very big one: up to 20 metres long, and with only very tiny and practically useless hind limbs.

Many thousands of fossils of different whale and proto-whale species have been found, so it's now possible to trace the ancestry of modern cetaceans to their origins. Geologist and anatomist William Flower, one of the first to suggest antecedents to the whales, proposed in 1883 that they were descended from a group of extinct ungulates called the mesonychids.[14] Even though modern whales don't have visible hind limbs, they do often have small remnant bones within the body and unattached to the skeleton which hint at their ancestry. Fowler linked these bones with the corresponding ones in the extinct animal group.

For many years, fossil finds of early whales tended to support Flowers's idea. Bones as well as teeth pointed in the direction of the mesonychids. The latest evidence, however, indicates rather that the cetaceans more likely arose from the mesonychids' sister group: the artiodactyls or even-toed ungulates.[15] In any case, both groups are ungulates and quite similar, apart from their toes; perhaps this doesn't matter so much, except to taxonomists with a special interest in these groups. That whales are descended from artiodactyls means, surprisingly, that their nearest modern-day relatives include giraffes, deer, pigs, and hippopotamuses. These conclusions, originally made by palaeontologists on anatomical grounds, have since been confirmed by DNA studies which also indicate that whales and hippos share a common ancestry.[16] There is hardly any finer proof of Darwin's theory of evolution.

Darwin's whale

Darwin also considered the evolution of whales. In order to illustrate how natural selection might work, he described in *On the Origin of Species* a hypothetical example of how evolution from a known animal could lead, if not to an actual whale, then to something *resembling* a whale. His example was based on observations made in the previous century by English explorer Samuel Hearne, who had worked for the Hudson's Bay Company in Canada. "In North America the black bear was seen by Hearne swimming for hours with widely open mouth, thus catching, like a whale, insects in the water. Even in so extreme a case as this, if the supply of insects were constant, and if better adapted competitors did not already exist in the country, I can see no difficulty in a race of bears being rendered, by natural selection, more and more aquatic in their structure and habits, with larger and larger mouths, till a creature was produced as monstrous as a whale".[17]

But few really understood what Darwin meant. Richard Owen thought he seriously believed that bears were the ancestors of whales— and mocked him publicly for it. In later editions, Darwin abandoned any attempt to explain the example further. He deleted the entire section, despite continuing to believe it was a valid example. "It is laughable how often I have been attacked and misrepresented about this Bear", he wrote.[18]

Darwin would certainly have been glad to know, as we do now, that whales actually did descend from as unlikely a group as the ungulates.

CHAPTER 10
Missing links

ALTHOUGH DARWIN SCARCELY mentioned the origins of mankind in *On the Origin of Species*, a heated exchange of opinions on this subject soon followed. His only comment on this was a vague allusion to the validity of applying the same reasoning to humankind as to animals: "Light will be thrown on the origin of man and his history".[1] But of course, he was not the only one thinking about this topic and its implications. Charles Lyell, for example, was also interested in human prehistory and was writing a book on the subject. Darwin commented in a letter to him: "You used to caution me to be cautious about man, I suspect I shall have to return the caution a hundred-fold!" With colleagues, Darwin could speak his mind. Leaving no doubt that he clearly understood that the ancestry of man went all the way back to the earliest of times and that man shared ancestry with all other living things, he added in a footnote: "Our ancestor was an animal which breathed water, had a swim-bladder, a great swimming tail, an imperfect skull & undoubtedly was an hermaphrodite! Here is a pleasant genealogy for mankind ...".[2]

But for now, Darwin confined his thoughts to private correspondence with like-minded friends and colleagues. That mankind should be a part of nature, subject to the same natural laws, and descended from the apes was too much for his contemporaries to swallow, he decided. However, he underestimated his contemporaries' ability to draw these conclusions from his theory by themselves.

Controversy: The descent of man

Despite avoiding arguments about this delicate subject, he could not prevent others from doing so. After publication of his book, lively exchanges about many aspects of Darwin's ideas ensued; however, no question was so heatedly debated, nor attracted so much attention, as that of the descent of mankind. Owen was one of his most prominent critics. According to him, there were such fundamental differences between brain structure in humans and in anthropoid apes that there could be no question of men being descended from apes. But Thomas Huxley—always ready for an argument, and especially with Owen—he had a telling riposte to offer. He pointed out that Owen himself had emphasised the similarities between man and apes in a scientific essay on mammals: "It is so rare a pleasure for me to find Professor Owen's opinions in entire concordance with my own, that I cannot forbear from quoting a paragraph which appeared in his essay".[3] The quotation he reproduced ran thus: "I cannot shut my eyes to the significance of that all-pervading similitude of structure – every tooth, every bone, strictly homologous – which makes the determination of the difference between *Homo* and *Pithecus* the anatomist's difficulty".

Huxley's point went home: even though Owen never acknowledged his mistake, he did remove the incriminating sentence from later editions of his essay. The argument raged on, culminating at the AGM of the British Association for the Advancement of Science at the Oxford University Museum in 1860. Bishop of Oxford Samuel

Wilberforce, a noted orator, delivered a broadside against supporters of evolution. In the ensuing debate, he asked Huxley sarcastically whether it was through his grandfather or his grandmother that he claimed descent from a monkey. Huxley, no doubt fired up by the heated atmosphere in the hall, replied that he was not ashamed to have a monkey for his ancestor; however, he would be ashamed to be connected to a man who used great gifts to obscure the truth. [4]. In the room, packed with an audience of over 800, there was great uproar. One woman fainted; Captain FitzRoy, of *Beagle* fame (who was there on the side of the traditionalists), hefted an enormous Bible and solemnly implored the audience to believe God rather than man. He also reportedly added his regret that he had ever taken Darwin aboard his ship and given him the chance to write such an immoral book as *On the Origin of Species*.

Darwin, as usual, was far from the scene himself. His intestines were troubling him terribly again, but he received news dispatches from his musketeers, who were all present for the debate. Hooker, in particular, offered a breathless description of feeling compelled to respond to Wilberforce's outburst and Huxley's defence (which, he feared, had been inaudible from the back of the hall and which, in any case, he thought lacked the intellectual depth of argument which he himself wished to offer). The night after the victory, he wrote to Darwin, describing the debate like a boxing match: "I hit him in the wind at the first shot in 10 words taken from his own ugly mouth — & then proceeded to demonstrate in as few more, 1 that he could never have read your book, & 2 that he was absolutely ignorant of the rudiments of Bot. Science".[5] No surprise that Wilberforce collapsed after such an attack.

The Descent of Man is published

After these initial quarrels, the dust settled. A decade later, the discussion had calmed down sufficiently that Darwin felt the time was right to speak out, so in 1871 he published *The Descent of Man*, in which he openly extended evolution by natural selection to include our own species. Yes, mankind is descended from the ape family, he said, and he laid out all the evidence supporting that claim. There were identical anatomical features, from the lack of a tail in anthropoid apes and the structure of the skull, to details of hair growth; there was behavioural evidence as well. One thing, however, was missing: there were no fossil remains of transitional forms which might illustrate how humans had evolved from their primate ancestors. Darwin never attempted to hide this fact; it was regrettable, he admitted, but "the discovery of fossil remains has been an extremely slow and fortuitous process. Nor should it be forgotten that those regions which are the most likely to afford remains connecting man with some extinct ape-like creature, have not as yet been searched by geologists".[6]

Darwin was the first to correctly guess that "those regions" were exactly where we should start looking for man's ancestors. He had found extinct giant sloths in South America in precisely the area where their modern day descendants still lived, so he applied the same logic now. "In each great region of the world, the living mammals are closely related to the extinct species of the same region. It is therefore probable that Africa was formerly inhabited by extinct apes closely allied to the gorilla and chimpanzee; and as these two species are now man's nearest allies, it is somewhat more probable that our early progenitors lived on the African continent than elsewhere".[7]

However, Darwin's advice went unheeded. Until the middle of the 20th century, conventional wisdom held that man's ancestors would be found in Asia, so why look in Africa? The only hominid fossils recognised up to this point came from Europe and Asia, so it seemed logical to continue the search there. True, some strangely large and heavy skulls had already been found in 1856 in Germany's Neander Valley, but the significance of these fossils was overlooked at first. Only later was it realised that the remains represented an extinct human species—named Neanderthal man.

In 1891, Dutch doctor Eugène Dubois unearthed in Java both a skullcap and a femur belonging to a new hominid species. However, only after similar finds had been made elsewhere, notably in China in the 1930s, did it receive its Latin name: *Homo erectus*, referring to its upright gait.

Nowadays, it is well documented that Darwin's supposition was correct: the cradle of mankind was indeed in Africa, and from there all hominid species emerged to colonise the world. This was established thanks largely to the Kenyan-British Leakey family and their work in East Africa, starting with palaeoanthropologist Louis Leakey and his wife Mary in the 1930s.

First hominid fossils in Africa

Before the Leakeys even began their explorations in Africa, a single but very exciting hominid skull had already been found there. It came into the hands of Raymond Dart, a young anthropologist in Johannesburg, thanks to the efforts of a colleague, Professor Robert Burns Young. In 1924, while visiting a limestone quarry in Taung, South Africa, geologist Young had noticed a skull on the desk of the quarry manager, where it was serving as a paperweight. He had promised Dart to keep an eye out for interesting specimens, so he packed up the skull, along with two boxes of other fossils from the same location, and sent them on to Dart in Johannesburg. About to leave for a wedding where he was to act as best man, Dart could not restrain his curiosity: He immediately broke open the cases where they stood in the driveway to his house.

"As soon as I removed the lid, a thrill of excitement shot through me. On the very top of the rock heap was what was undoubtedly an endocranial cast or mould of the interior of the skull. Had it been only the fossilised brain cast of any species of ape, it would have been ranked as a great discovery, for such a thing had never before been reported. But I knew at a glance that what lay in my hands was no ordinary anthropoidal brain. Here, in lime-consolidated sand, was the replica of a brain three times as large as that of a baboon and considerably bigger than that of any adult chimpanzee." Dart knew immediately that he had something incredibly valuable in his hands. "I stood in the shade, holding the brain as greedily as any miser hugs his gold, my mind racing ahead. Here, I was certain, was one of the most significant finds ever made in the history of anthropology. Darwin's largely discredited theory that man's early progenitors probably lived in Africa came back to me. Was I to be the instrument by which his 'missing link' was found?"[8] Dart was interrupted by the bridegroom, telling him the car was on its way to take them to the church; but of course, he rushed back afterwards to take a closer look.

Part of the fossil was embedded in limestone, so Dart had to carefully chip it out—using his wife's knitting needles, which he filed to a sharp point. Once this slow task was finished and his analysis completed, he published his discovery in the journal *Nature*. The skull had many more traits in common with the skulls of modern humans than with those of apes, although the brain volume was significantly smaller than in modern man. It appeared to belong to a young child—the molars were about to break through—so Dart judged it to be the skull of someone about six years old. He called the new species *Australopithecus africanus,* meaning "the southern ape from Africa", although this specimen is often referred to as the Taung child. Dart predicted that many more fossils were to be found in Southern Africa which would help clarify the evolution of mankind.[9]

However, Dart's sensational discovery did not receive the acclaim he might have hoped for. Dart was an outsider; also, the orthodox place to expect hominid fossils at that time was in the Far East. Most other anthropologists viewed the Taung fossil as that of an ape, a baboon, or a gorilla. Frustrated, Dart brought the skull to a scientific congress in England. On the way, disaster struck when Dart's wife left the skull in its box on the back seat of a London taxi. Discovering it later, the understandably shocked driver handed it in at a police station, and it was returned safely to Dart. However, for 20 years his discovery would continue to be ignored by the establishment.

The Leakeys in Africa

Meanwhile, the doyen of English palaeontologists had begun his work in Africa. Louis Leakey had grown up in Kenya, studied in England, and then returned to his beloved homeland with his wife Mary. From the 1930s onwards, he—and, in time, Mary—dedicated his life to the search for fossils and stone tools belonging to mankind's ancestors in Kenya and Tanzania. And they did find them—not immediately and not consistently, but at long intervals, with much hard work and disappointment in between. In fact, it is amazing that they even continued the search, considering how many barren years they had to persist through. Nevertheless, in 1948, by the shores of Lake Victoria, the couple unearthed a nearly complete skull of a very early anthropoid ape which they identified as *Proconsul africanus*. The skull shows some human-like traits; for example, it lacks the prominent eyebrow ridge seen in the great apes. But other factors, such as the teeth, are more ape-like, and other specimens found indicated that *Proconsul* did not walk upright on the ground but lived in the trees.

Both Louis and Mary Leakey found great numbers of fossil bones. Often, though, they would dig out just a single tooth or a small fragment of a jawbone. If you, like most of us, cannot distinguish a pig's jaw from a deer's, you might wonder how anything at all can be deduced from such small remains. However, if you know what to look for, ape and human bones are not so hard to tell apart. For example, the human jawbone is parabolic in shape, whereas in the chimpanzee and gorilla it is narrower and more rectangular with almost parallel sides. With regard to teeth, human canines are small and rounded by comparison with those of the apes; also, they are held vertically within the jaw rather than slanting outwards, as in the apes. Even the tooth enamel is different: a relatively thin layer in the apes, but very thick in humans.

Eventually, the Leakeys did find more than fragments. Their great breakthrough came in 1959, after 24 seasons of fieldwork in the Olduvai Gorge in Tanzania, when Mary Leakey found a fine skull which was unmistakably hominid.[10] Not a human skull, then, but from one of the other species in our lineage dating from the time after the divergence from the apes. Mary Leakey's fossil has since been reclassified several times and is now called *Australopithecus boisei*—a name showing its relation to the Taung child from South Africa, also an *Australopithecus*. This discovery convinced the wider world that East Africa was indeed the place to look for fossils of early man; as a result, palaeontologists from all over the world have since then been a more or less constant presence in the region.

Lucy and Toumaï

Another major find was made in 1974 when American anthropologist Donald Johanson uncovered the most complete skeleton of an early hominid to date, this time in Ethiopia. Astonishingly, this was not just a fragment of a skull or a femur but rather several hundred pieces, including large parts of the pelvis, rib cage, and spinal column as well as arm and leg bones. In fact, as much as 40 percent of the fossilised skeleton was recovered, making a complete reconstruction possible for the first time. In describing the find, Johanson labelled it A.L. 288–1 and gave it the species name *Australopithecus afarensis.*[11] Privately, however, he used the same name that the rest of the world came to use: Lucy. One member of the expedition party thought of this name after the Beatles song *Lucy in the Sky with Diamonds* had been played in camp more or less continuously on the night of the discovery.

Lucy was an exciting and important find in many ways, but perhaps the most significant fact—which Johanson and his colleagues could immediately determine—was that "she" had walked upright on two legs. They could tell this from the orientation of the pelvis and femur, which was very different from that of animals that go on all fours. Lucy would have stood only about 105 centimetres tall, and her brain was not so big: only about 400 cubic centimetres, which is a long way from the 1400 cubic centimetres which an average adult human brain is equipped with today. From this, we deduce that upright walking preceded development of a large brain.

Lucy was not only the most complete hominid skeleton at the time of discovery but also the oldest. The bones were dated to about 3.2 million years old, a record which wasn't beaten for another 20 years. We now have several older finds, including a remarkable example from the Sahel region of Chad, where the current record-holder was unearthed in 2002 by Michel Brunet and his team. *Sahelanthropus tchadensis* is not just a little older but also twice as ancient as Lucy—roughly 7 million years old. Like Lucy, this fossil was given a pet name, Toumaï, which is a little easier to pronounce than the Latin name. Toumaï has both very primitive features and more advanced ones. In particular, the fossil lacks the prominent canines of a chimpanzee, and the foramen magnum (the hole at the base of the skull through which the spinal cord passes) is shifted forward, as is seen in bipedal hominids such as *Australopithecus* and *Homo*. Its brain case, however, is very small. Taking all these points together, Brunet concludes that Toumaï is in the hominid lineage, but very close to the point where it split from the chimpanzee line.[12]

Out of Africa

With more than 1,000 fossils of prehistoric humans, apes, and hominids discovered thus far in Africa, no one today doubts that it was here that mankind arose. The point of divergence, when the early hominids separated from the other apes, is believed to lie about 7 or 8 million years ago. Although humans have many traits in common with chimpanzees—and indeed share with them large parts of our DNA—that doesn't mean we are descended from them. The chimpanzee species we know today were not alive 7 to 8 million years ago. Unfortunately, no fossils exist to tell us anything about the evolution of chimpanzees—for the simple reason that chimps are, and always have been, animals of the rainforest, where it's extremely unlikely for a dead animal to end up being fossilised.

We also know that several species of hominids lived side by side on the African continent. For millions of years hominids were confined to Africa, but fossil remains show that members of at least one species, *Homo erectus,* emigrated from Africa and established themselves in Eurasia. These remains have been found on Java and in Beijing and several European locations. However, only one band of *Homo erectus* went this way; other fossils from all over Africa show the same species still living on their home continent throughout the same periods.

In time though, the species disappeared from both Asia and Africa at the same time that another species of early humans emerged from Africa to establish itself in Europe and Asia about 400,000 years ago. This time, it was *Homo heidelbergensis* on the rise—a robust species of humans well known from numerous, mostly European fossils. The first *Homo heidelbergensis* fossil was found near Heidelberg, Germany; however, the species is also known from Africa and is believed to have originated there, like all other human species. *Homo heidelbergensis* may be the ancestor of *Homo neanderthalensis*. If so, that would explain why Neanderthal fossils are found only in Europe.

The first fossilised skulls of early humans were actually found in Darwin's lifetime, in a cave in Belgium in 1829 and in a quarry in Gibraltar in 1848. The earlier find was correctly identified as human and very ancient—but no one imagined how ancient, and there were no good ways of dating fossils at that time. The skull from Gibraltar also went unremarked for a while. But in 1856, matching bones were found in the Neander Valley in southern Germany, and Johann Fuhlrott recognised them as belonging to a new species. After the name *Homo neanderthalensis* was coined in 1864, all the bones were assigned to the same species.

If we compare the Neanderthal fossils with the many hominid fossils from Africa, two important points emerge. First, "Neanderthal man" was not just a hominid; he belonged to the same genus as we do: *Homo*. In other words, he was a human, not an ape. Second, compared with our distant ancestors in Africa, Neanderthal man was here just the day before yesterday. The last Neanderthals died out only about 40,000 years ago—very recently, compared with the time scales we use when describing hominids in Africa. There is no doubt that Neanderthals and modern man, *Homo sapiens*, coexisted in Europe for thousands of years. How they got on with each other is a question we can't yet answer. Hypotheses range from the idea that Neanderthals were actively wiped out by *Homo sapiens* to the idea that there may have been interbreeding between the two species during a gradual process of domination. The tribe of *Homo sapiens* which the Neanderthals encountered (and from which all living human beings today are descended) represented the last of a series of migrations out of Africa. This migration, it is believed, took place less than 100,000 years ago, after *Homo sapiens* had already lived in Africa for several million years. The timing of this last great exodus—which led to mankind's colonising the entire Earth—has been established not by fossil evidence but by comparing DNA from different ethnic groups worldwide.

Piltdown man

Perhaps the most infamous fossil story—and one which certainly damaged the credibility of science in general and evolutionary theory in particular—concerned the skull of "Piltdown man", named after the gravel pit in Sussex from which the find was reported in 1912. The discovery was an immediate sensation, and the skull was promptly acquired for the prestigious Museum of Natural History in London, where it was treasured as a priceless relic for over 40 years. At that time, no other early human fossils had been found in continental Europe apart from the Neanderthals, so Piltdown man acquired enormous scientific importance. The skull was very human-looking and in the same proportions as a modern *Homo sapiens*, while the primitive-looking jaws and teeth revealed that this prehistoric individual had a number of ape-like characteristics. There was good reason for that, as the world learned in 1953, when Piltdown man was shown to be a complete forgery. The skull looked "modern human" because it was indeed a modern human's, while the ape-like jaws came from an orang-utang!

The admission that their experts had been duped was highly embarrassing for the Museum, and it also meant that the authenticity of many other valuable finds was called into question. Even today, some websites try to persuade their readers that the *Archaeopteryx* from Germany is nothing more than a clever fake—created by proponents of evolutionary theory to provide evidence for their ideas.

Piltdown man was also one of the reasons why Raymond Dart found it so difficult to get anyone interested in his Taung child from South Africa. British palaeontologists already had their own skull, and it no doubt suited many of them much better to believe that their ancestors had lived in the Sussex countryside rather than in black Africa!

The question of questions for mankind

The fossil record is no longer blank when it comes to human ancestors. On the contrary: during the past 50 years, a wealth of remains has been identified in Africa, both of early humans and of older hominids in our evolutionary line. Some are known only from a single find; others, from many. As in Darwin's day, there are plenty of disagreements (but, fortunately, not so much enmity) about how the finds should be interpreted. For example, the number of species represented by the fossils we have remains a matter of dispute: were there really so many different hominids, or was there simply a lot of variation within the species? Or sometimes a find is reclassified under a different name when someone determines that it belongs to an already-described species. There is also much debate regarding which species are close to the direct line of evolution of our human species and which are out on side branches.

In other words, anyone looking for an area of research with plenty of questions to answer for years to come would find the field of human evolution to be at least as exciting a choice today as it was 125 years ago. As Huxley wrote in the introduction to his essay on the relationship of mankind to the lower animals: "The question of questions for mankind—the problem which underlies all others, and is more deeply interesting than any other—is the ascertainment of the place which Man occupies in nature and of his relations to the universe of things".[13]

CHAPTER 11

The last piece in the puzzle

As DARWIN PUT together the jigsaw puzzle of the origin of species, he recognised that he was missing a piece. The entire edifice depended on the inheritance of characteristics from one generation to the next, but he had no good explanation for how this might actually happen. Years of experimentation with crossing plants and breeding doves, as well as a lifetime of correspondence with experts and experimenters all over the world, had not brought him any closer to an answer.

That certain traits were somehow inherited, there was no doubt—for on what other principle was plant and animal breeding based? Or, as Darwin asked, "What can be more wonderful than the well-ascertained fact that the minute ovule of a good milking cow will produce a male, from whom a cell, in union with an ovule, will produce a female, and she, when mature, will have large mammary glands, yielding an abundant supply of milk, and even milk of a particular quality?"[1] The willingness of breeders to pay good money for breeding animals also bore witness to the general agreement that traits were indeed inherited.

In the private sphere, Darwin also thought he observed the workings of heredity. "My eldest boy is showing the hereditary principle, by a passion for collecting Lepidoptera [butterflies]",[2] he writes proudly to his cousin William Fox. But otherwise, he was more concerned about the negative effects of heredity in relation to his children. In another letter to his cousin, he recalls the good old days of their student years at Cambridge: "What pleasant times we had in drinking Coffee in your rooms at Christ Coll ... Ah in those days there were no professions for sons, no ill-health to fear for them, no Californian gold—no French invasions. How paramount the future is to the present, when one is surrounded by children. My dread is hereditary ill-health. Even death is better for them",[3] he writes sombrely in the midst of an otherwise light-hearted letter.

Critique of the idea of heredity

One Darwin critic in particular tackled the problem of heredity—Fleeming Jenkin, professor of engineering at Edinburgh University. Almost ten years after the publication of *On the Origin of Species*, he wrote a review and critique of the book and of the ideas which Darwin stood for. Jenkin commented, with a touch of dry humour: "That theory rests on the assumption that natural selection can do slowly what man's selection does quickly; it is by showing how much man can do, that Darwin hopes to prove how much can be done without him".[4] Jenkin challenged the conclusion that new species can arise if given enough time, simply on the basis that (according to Darwin) a certain Sir John Sebright took six years to breed a special kind of dove. "This seems no more accurate than to conclude that because we observe that a cannon-ball has traversed a mile in a minute, therefore in an hour it will be sixty miles off, and in the course of ages that it will reach the fixed stars", he remarked drily.

Jenkin objected in particular to the fact that the entire theory depends on the inheritance of spontaneously generated variations within species. He saw as problematic the fact that inherited traits are often not preserved in their "pure" form. "Suppose a white man to have been wrecked on an island inhabited by negroes …", he wrote, "… there does not follow the conclusion that, after a limited or unlimited number of generations, the inhabitants of the island will be white".[5]

At a time when the British Empire was at its height, Jenkin had no problem imagining that a single white man would subdue the island's black inhabitants, slaughter a few, take a number of wives, and father many children. Still, even with the manifest "superiority" of the white race, he cannot imagine that it will result in subsequent inhabitants of the island all becoming white. Darwin recognised that he had a point. If in fact inheritance works like pouring milk into coffee—in that mixing two sets of inherited characteristics simply results in a dilution of both—then it's hard to fit in the idea of selection.

Pangenesis

Jenkin's argument was a hard nut for Darwin to crack, and he never managed it. His best shot at a theory of inheritance was something he called "pangenesis"; according to this theory, every cell in the body holds tiny grains or buds ("gemmules") which contain the hereditary material. Gemmules are transferred from parents to offspring, wandering through the body until they find the place where they belong. There, they develop into cells similar to the ones they came from, with the appropriate characteristics. Gemmules can also enter into a latent state, with the inherited traits emerging only later in life—as with some hereditary diseases—or even several generations later.

With pangenesis, Darwin was closely approaching Lamarckism, something he had always tried to avoid. One problematic implication of the theory is that, if you cut off a mouse's tail, there will be no tail gemmules to be transferred to a new individual and therefore no tails in the offspring. It is, of course, easy to demonstrate that inheritance does not work this way—assuming you have no objection to cutting tails off mice. German biologist August Weismann had no problem with this; he proceeded to remove 1,500 mouse tails in an 1888 experiment which was entirely successful in disproving Darwin's conjecture.

Darwin's theory of pangenesis is also unable to explain how reproduction sometimes leads to a mixing of characteristics, as in Jenkin's example, and sometimes to the inheritance of significant traits in a pure form. All this and more would be explained by a contemporary of Darwin, but Darwin died without ever having heard of him or his observations and conclusions.

The silent monk

This unknown fellow, Gregor Mendel, lived the quiet life of an Augustinian friar at a monastery in Brno, then in Austria and now in the Czech Republic. Mendel studied philosophy and physics at the University of Vienna and trained as teacher, but he dedicated himself to the experimental gardens in his charge at the monastery. He was particularly interested in cross-breeding plants in order to produce strains with desired characteristics. His speciality was ordinary garden peas. One secret to the success of his experiments was that he started with carefully selected and pure lines which he knew would breed true: that is, a pea with red flowers would produce seeds that also grew into peas with red flowers, and a wrinkled-seeded pea would never start producing round peas. Mendel chose seven traits in all, beginning by crossing the different lines with each other: a red-flowered plant with a white-flowered plant, a tall-growing plant with a low-growing one, a wrinkled-seeded plant with a round-seeded one. He hand-pollinated all the flowers himself, using a small paintbrush, and covered the flowers with small bags for the duration of the trials to ensure that bees and other insects would not destroy his experiments.

He recorded very conscientiously the traits of each succeeding generation of the plants, their flowers, and their seeds.

If Mendel had followed this procedure with only a few dozen plants, he would not have been able to discern any patterns in the results. But he was a thorough and patient man. He bred hundreds of plants year after year, using in total over 18,000 plants. As a result, he found clear patterns in the way characteristics were passed on down through the generations. If, dear reader, you have long forgotten Mendel's Laws of Inheritance from your school biology lessons, let us now remind you. The diligent monk found that different traits were inherited to different degrees: what he called "dominant" traits were three times as likely as "recessive" traits to appear in the second generation. Moreover, he determined that for each trait in an offspring, one-half was inherited from each parent. We now know that this holds true for all living organisms. For each inheritable characteristic or trait we possess, we have inherited one half from our fathers and one half from our mothers. The word "gene" had not yet been coined, but this is what we are talking about.

Mendel and Darwin

Mendel had probably read Darwin or was at least familiar with his ideas and conclusions. *On the Origin of Species* had been published in German in 1860, only a year after its publication in England. Even so, Mendel commented in his paper that it had often been claimed that cultivated species exhibited less stability than wild ones. In other words, Darwin (or others) may well have shown that cultivated species can change very rapidly by means of artificial selection, but that wild species are more stable. However, Mendel could not understand why moving a wild plant into a garden would cause it to suddenly start functioning in an entirely different way. "No one will seriously maintain that in the open country the development of plants is ruled by other laws than in the garden bed",[6] he writes.

Unfortunately, Darwin's theory in need of a mechanism and Mendel's explanation of that mechanism of heredity were destined to pass each other like ships in the night. Mendel did present his discoveries to the public in 1865, but only at the local Natural History Society of Brno—not exactly the British Association for the Advancement of Science. His lectures were spread over two evenings (he had a lot to say), but there was little response. The following year, the comprehensive manuscript on which the lectures had been based was published, and Mendel sent copies to various botanists he knew. None of his readers appears to have been able to see what was so revolutionary in his experiments—or perhaps they got bogged down in the mass of details Mendel included. After Mendel's death in 1884, his epoch-making discoveries were quietly forgotten.

Only at the beginning of the 20th century was his manuscript "rediscovered" and translated into English. Even then, however, Mendel's discovery of the laws of inheritance did not, as one might expect, mean that Darwin's theory would finally be accepted. Since publication of *On the Origin of Species*, there had definitely been increasing acceptance of evolution as such—but not of its mechanism, natural selection. For a long time, Mendel's laws of inheritance were interpreted as a sort of "either-or" rule (flowers will be either red or white, peas will be either round or wrinkled), allowing little room to explain the small and gradual variations which Darwin had described as the basis of the operation of natural selection.

Modern synthesis

Although the late 19th and early 20th centuries saw gradual acceptance of evolution as such, natural selection faded away as an explanation for the mechanism driving the process. It was first revived with the advent of what was termed the "new synthesis" or the "modern synthesis". This linking of Darwin and Mendel also managed to explain something neither of them alone could account for: namely, the blending of characteristics referred to in Jenkin's example of the stranded sailor and his mixed-race offspring. The explanation was that some factors (for example, those determining eye colour or shape of the ear lobe) are passed on by a single gene and therefore follow Mendel's laws. We owe other traits, such as skin colour, to several different genes; each of these separately still follows Mendelian inheritance, but the combined effect is a mixture which does not.

A key contributor to the modern evolutionary synthesis was the Englishman Ronald Fisher, not only a biologist and geneticist but also a statistician of the first rank. Amongst a number of his crucial insights, a major success was his use of mathematics to prove that natural selection could operate on small variations over a realistic time scale. He even showed that smaller variations are actually the most suitable for natural selection to operate on, because they are more likely than large variations to survive for several generations. Other scientists were drawn to the field, and in the course of two decades, new understandings about genetics and inheritance were added to Darwin's theories—creating what became known as neo-Darwinism. Leading lights in this colourful field included J.B.S. Haldane, Sewall Wright, Ernst Mayr, and Theo Dobzhansky.

Haldane in particular lived up to the classic image of the slightly crazy scientific genius with a highly eccentric lifestyle. A non-believer and Marxist (who became a member of the Communist party), he was once asked what, as a scientist, he could deduce about the nature of God by studying His creation. Haldane (who knew that about half of all species on Earth were beetles) is said to have replied laconically that the only thing he could deduce was that God must have had an inordinate fondness for beetles.

In a book review published in 1963, Haldane wrote that it would in theory be possible to clone human cells, something he thought would be an excellent idea because of the impracticality of experimenting on identical twins.[7] In another book review the same year, he speculated about how the book's conclusions would be received, imagining that the process of acceptance will follow the "usual four stages: (i) This is worthless nonsense; (ii) This is an interesting, but perverse, point of view; (iii) This is true, but quite unimportant; (iv) I always said so".[8]

The same could be said about the reception of Darwin's theory of evolution.

Discovery of the structure of DNA

The next breakthrough in research into genetics came in the 1950s, when Watson and Crick described the structure of DNA. For some time, it had been known that DNA was the material responsible for transmission of inherited characteristics, but there was no real understanding of how it worked or what its structure was. It was impossible to understand that a molecule known to consist of just sugars, phosphates, and four different nitrogenous bases could be responsible for transmitting all the inherited variation existing in life on Earth.

Watson and Crick posited that DNA, though a large molecule, had a very simple structure similar to a twisting spiral staircase in which the stringers consisted of the sugar molecules and the steps of the nitrogenous bases. A major help in revealing this pattern was provided by the technique of X-ray crystallography. An x-ray, having a shorter wavelength than ordinary light, can resolve structures on a molecular level which cannot be perceived by means of light. The x-ray pictures were taken by Rosalind Franklin, working at a rival laboratory at King's College, London, and shown to Watson and Crick without her knowledge. But it was Watson and Crick who realised, as soon as they saw a single one of Franklin's pictures, that they were looking at a spiral structure. (This shows up in two dimensions as an x-shaped pattern.) Watson and Crick immediately began building a Meccano-like model to see how the known chemical components of DNA could fit into a helical structure; this became the famous double helix.

In 1953, they published their proposed structure of DNA in the prestigious journal *Nature*. It was one of the shortest papers in the history of science—just a single page. The discovery was more than enough, however, to earn the pair their Nobel Prize in 1962.

Many issues relating to inheritance became much clearer with Watson and Crick's discovery. Our genes are responsible for producing all possible kinds of proteins having innumerable functions within the cells of the body. DNA consists of an incredibly long chain of base pairs attached to the sugar-phosphate backbone holding it all together. A gene is a specific segment of this chain, containing from thousands to millions of base pairs and representing the actual unit of inheritance. The bases come in four varieties and are used to make up code sequences which in turn determine precisely which amino acids are combined together in protein synthesis. It's the sheer number of possible lengths of segments and combinations of base pairs on the DNA string which makes it possible to build all types of proteins— thus producing the inheritable variations we see, even with a code composed of only four units.

Whether the segment of DNA we call a gene is short or long, the base sequence always codes for the synthesis of a particular protein—a simple one requiring fewer units of code than a complex one. If a piece of the gene is missing (or a bit has been added or changed from the normal sequence) then a different protein will be manufactured by the cells. Such changes in DNA give rise to so-called mutations. They can arise spontaneously or can be caused by exterior agents such as ultraviolet irradiation. We all have numerous mutations in our genetic material, and this doesn't necessarily mean much. In fact, it's one reason why we are all different. However, some mutations are very damaging and can have serious consequences.

Tree of life

The discovery of DNA has revolutionised our understanding of not only genetics but also how evolution works. An important field within biology is concerned with constructing genealogical trees for animals and plants—what taxonomists call phylogenies. Of course, we had those before the discovery of DNA, and physical characteristics such as the form of teeth, jaws, or bones (or, in plants, the structure of flowers) can still be used to determine whether two species are closely or distantly related. One of the first to suggest a genealogical tree for all life on Earth was German zoologist Ernst Haeckel, a great admirer of Darwin. Some of his genealogical drawings resembled real trees with thick trunks (oak trees, in fact), with the "lower" animals down near the roots and man right at the top.

For fossils, which don't contain DNA, physical characteristics are still the only ones we have to go on in order to decide, for example, where to place a new find of hominid remains from Africa on the genealogical tree. As with physical characteristics, genealogical tables based on DNA samples are arranged according to the degrees of similarity between the organisms being compared. The assumption is that the more closely related two organisms are, the more agreement there will be between their DNA. Thus we can build phylogenetic trees for different groups of animals and plants in the same way, simply by analysing their DNA.

Modern diagrams of genealogical relationships of life on Earth no longer resemble Haeckel's oak trees very much. They have no crown and no trunk and are more like a large sphere from which life evolves in all directions. The origins of life are to be found at the centre of the sphere, whereas on the surface we see all extant forms of life— whether bacteria, algae, fungi, plants, or animals. All are the successful offspring of their ancestral forms.

Genealogy of seals and sea lions

For many years, controversy raged over the origins of seals and sea lions and the relationship between these two groups of similar-looking marine mammals. This was perhaps not a controversy which kept the general public awake at nights, but still a battle fought at numerous conferences and in scientific publications. On the one side were those who held that sea lions differed so greatly from seals that each group must have originated from a separate group of terrestrial predators. Sea lions must have descended from bears, they said: they can almost walk on their hind limbs, they have visible outer ears, and they exhibit extreme sexual dimorphism (males being much larger than females). Seals, on the other hand, must have descended from the same group as martens. On the other side were biologists and systematists who thought that, with so many similarities between sea lions and seals, they must have common origins; they thought that both would probably have been close to martens.

The argument has continued for many decades but seems to be finally drawing to a close. Isabelle Delisle and Curtis Strobeck at the University of Edmonton in Canada have compared DNA from a large number of predators; their results indicate it's highly probable that seals and sea lions do have common origins.[9] Still, they aren't quite sure whether their common ancestors were bears or martens—so the discussion is perhaps not quite over....

DNA bar codes

Another technique made possible by the discovery of DNA is so-called DNA bar coding. In principle, it's possible to recognise the species of an organism from its DNA alone—you don't need to see the actual plant or animal. What's more, you need only to check a very short section of the DNA code, typically a defined region of known inter-species variability. This means the old-school ornithologist with his binoculars and the butterfly hunter with his net now face competition from a very new kind of biologist, one who can pin down a species from microscopic samples in a test tube. The technique makes it possible to determine which species are present in a locality and whether they are unknown species. Once the relevant species' DNA bar codes are in a database, scientists worldwide can check a species they have found against the database—instead of having to undertake an extensive literature search or visits to museums in order to identify it.

Since DNA analysis requires only a few cells of material to identify a species, it also opens up the exciting possibility of simply using soil or water samples to see which animals have inhabited a given locality—without anyone needing to see the actual animals or disturb them in any way.

Evolution and DNA

The discovery of DNA and the formulation of laws of inheritance have had enormous significance for the understanding of how evolution works. It has become much more feasible to test different hypotheses, both about the common origins of all organisms and about how natural selection operates in nature. And we now understand that mechanisms other than natural selection can be at play in the creation of new species.

Much as Darwin would have been delighted with the millions of fossils dug up within the past 100 years, and with the support these have given to his theory of evolution, he would be no less pleased with the developments that have taken place in the field of genetics.

CHAPTER 12

From orchids to orcas

As DARWIN GOT older, he threw himself more and more into studying plants. At the bottom of his garden, he had a small greenhouse built to the latest design, with a heating system and tables for the plants to stand on. Naturally, the plants came from Hooker; by now, he had become director of the Royal Botanical Gardens at Kew, which already housed the largest collection of plants in the world. "The Plants arrived quite safe last night", Darwin wrote eagerly in thanks. "I am fairly astounded at their number! why, my hot-house is almost full! — I have not yet even looked out [*sic*] their names; but I can see several things which I wished for, but which I did not like to ask for".[1] Among the plants Hooker sent was a collection of orchids, a plant family which interested Darwin very much.

Darwin's orchid

One reason orchids are exciting is that they are adapted for pollination by insects, often in such a specialised way that a given species of orchid is entirely dependent on a specific insect to pollinate it. Like many flowers, orchids produce nectar. Nectar has no significance for the flowers other than being a sweetly scented, sugary liquid—which is a good way of attracting insects. When they visit a flower, insects pick up some of its pollen on their bodies and carry this to the next flower; fertilisation occurs when the pollen touches the stigma of the second flower.

As was his custom, Darwin pumped everyone he knew for information. James Bateman, a wealthy Staffordshire horticulturalist and orchid collector, was happy to help. "Though by no means a convert to your theory as to the 'Origin of Species', I wish the matter to be thoroughly ventilated ...",[2] he wrote to Darwin. To show his friendliness, he also sent Darwin a box full of some exceptionally beautiful orchids from Madagascar.

These orchids produced large, waxy, white flowers with nectaries in the form of extremely long tubes, up to a foot (30 centimetres) long in fact. Darwin observed that nectar appeared only in the bottom two inches of the nectary. The flower seemed so strange that Darwin promptly reported back to Hooker: "I have just received such a Box full from Mr Bateman with the astounding *Angræcum sesquipedale* with a nectary a foot long", he wrote, adding thoughtfully: "Good Heavens what insect can suck it?"[3] Darwin soon answered his own question. Since the nectary was so long, there had to exist on Madagascar a moth or butterfly with a proboscis equally long, which could reach to the bottom of it to obtain the nectar. Otherwise, the orchid could not be fertilised.

The problem was, no such moth had ever been found on Madagascar. Darwin was not concerned; Madagascar was a big place, the moth would be there somewhere. He was also supported by Wallace, who was equally convinced that the moth had to exist. "That such a moth exists in Madagascar may be safely predicted; and naturalists who visit that island should search for it with as much confidence as astronomers searched for the planet Neptune,—and I venture to predict they will be equally successful!"[4] he wrote. And of course, it *was* there—although Darwin would not live to see it.

In 1903, just such a moth, with a 30-centimetre-long proboscis, was found in the Madagascar forests. It was named *Xanthopan morganii praedicta* ("*praedicta*" out of respect for Wallace, who had predicted its existence so long before).

The phenomenon Darwin described regarding the orchid and the moth is called co-evolution. The term describes what happens when different organisms evolve in relation to each other—whether as competitors, for example, or as "collaborators", as with flowers and their pollinators. Co-evolution has become an important field of research in recent decades.

The tropics are replete with examples of co-evolution between animals and plants. For example, not just moths have evolved alongside flowers; many nectar-eating bats are also important pollinators. Nathan Muchhala of the University of Miami (Florida), following in Darwin's footsteps, discovered a species of bat also specialised in extracting nectar from flowers with hard-to-reach nectaries. The flower in question is long and funnel-shaped and can be pollinated only by a single species of bat, the barely six-centimetres-long, tube-lipped nectar bat *Anoura fistulata*. In relation to its body size, this tiny bat has the longest tongue of any mammal, stretching to half as long again as its own body. When the tongue is not in use, the nectar bat stows it in its throat and between its ribs, which are specially adapted for this purpose.[5]

Genetic drift

Co-evolution is only one of many areas of research within contemporary evolutionary biology. The revival of Darwinism, beginning in the 1920s, led to new interest in demonstrating evolution in practice and in applying the new understanding of how genes operate to studies of animal and plant populations. It also meant that natural selection was no longer seen as the only mechanism affecting evolution.

Most evolutionary biologists agree that natural selection is an important mechanism in the evolution of new species. However, they have also observed another, more random process which may affect evolution: so-called "genetic drift".

In a large population, variations due to chance will soon cancel each other out. If we imagine a pond inhabited by a hypothetical species of frog which comes in two varieties, blue-spotted and green-spotted, and if there is no advantage in terms of natural selection to either colour scheme, we can expect to find roughly equal amounts of blue-spotted and green-spotted frogs in the pool when we sample it. There may be variations from year to year: in some years, more blue-spotted frogs may be predated, compared to the green-spotted ones, and in some years more blue-spotted tadpoles may survive to adulthood than green-spotted ones. But because the pond is large and contains lots of frogs, and because the variations are small, the distribution will eventually be stabilised again.

On the other hand, if we imagine a much smaller pond containing very few frogs—ten of each colour, for example—then even small chance events may affect the future relative abundance of the green- or blue-spotted variants. If a hungry heron eats ten frogs, and by chance seven of them are blue-spotted (the remaining frogs are green-spotted), the balance of the population in the pond has been altered to the extent that now more than twice as many of the one sort remain as the other. Note that this happens entirely by chance: if blue spots on frogs made them easier for herons to find in a pool with lots of green vegetation, then herons would eat more of the blue-spotted than the green-spotted frogs. In this example, however, we would say that the uneven distribution arose as the result of natural selection. Suppose now that some children come along to catch frogs for their aquarium and happen to get two more blue-spotted frogs: now the future breeding population is down to one blue-spotted and seven green-spotted frogs. This proportion will strongly affect colour distribution in future generations.

Biologists call this mechanism "genetic drift". It differs fundamentally from natural selection in that it is attributed to purely chance events. In any population, and especially in a small one, there is risk that random circumstances may determine which individuals will survive to reproduce—and it's equally fortuitous which *kinds* of individuals will survive. In other words, genetic drift can drive evolution. Initially, it may cause a population in a certain area to acquire slightly different traits or a slightly different appearance from other members of the species elsewhere, but ultimately it can be a factor in the creation of entirely new species.

Population bottlenecks

An extreme case of genetic drift is seen when populations of animals or plants experience what biologists call a genetic "bottleneck". This is observed when, at some point in the past, a population has sunk so low that only a few individuals have survived to reproduce; they have then become the ancestors of a subsequent population expansion. Such a bottleneck is visible in a modern population when genetic variation or diversity is much lower than one would expect for a population of that size. Low diversity arises because the population has descended from just a few individuals bearing whatever genes they happened to have.

Such a genetic bottleneck has been deduced in the case of the cheetah. Fifteen thousand years ago, cheetahs were widespread across Africa and large parts of Asia. Today, cheetahs are largely confined to East Africa and parts of south-west Africa, in addition to a critically endangered sub-population of fewer than 100 animals in Iran.

Recent population estimates worldwide are between 7,000 and 10,000 cheetahs remaining, all of them genetically so similar that one could transplant skin from one animal to any other without risk of rejection.[6] This close genetic similarity indicates that at some time, cheetahs passed through a population bottleneck which only a tiny number of individuals survived.

Because cheetahs are endangered and furthermore very difficult to breed in captivity, scientists have closely investigated their genetic makeup in an attempt to avoid further inbreeding. DNA analysis of cheetahs alive today makes it possible to calculate that the population bottleneck happened more than 10,000 years ago, at about the same time as other mass extinctions affecting large mammals all over the world.[7]

Many other animals and plants experienced such a bottleneck. For elephant seals, the bottleneck occurred roughly 100 years ago, when the northern elephant seal was hunted to the brink of extinction. It has been estimated that by 1890, there were fewer than 100 left. Today, they have spread back up the western coast of North America, and their population is estimated to be over 100,000 and growing. However, because they are all descended from the same small group of 19th-century survivors, their genetic diversity is very low—not unlike that of some types of inbred domestic animals.

At present, low genetic diversity doesn't seem to be creating any problems in the wild, either for cheetahs or for elephant seals. The fear is, however, that low diversity makes it easier for these species to be overwhelmed by disease or environmental changes. With epidemic disease, a segment of a normally diverse population remains unaffected while many other individuals become sick and die. (The assumption is that the unaffected individuals have a genetically determined immunity to the disease.) Given that cheetah and elephant seal populations lack genetic diversity, they could be very severely impacted by epidemics or environmental changes.

A special case of the bottleneck effect is seen in situations where a small fraction of the total population becomes the nucleus of a new population. Plant seeds may wash up on an island and begin to germinate there, or a flock of birds may be carried off course and establish a colony in a new area. Over a long period of time, by a combination of genetic drift and natural selection, this may lead to the formation of a new species.

White bears

The theory of evolution is very much about how new species are formed, but it gives us an overall picture rather than detailed mechanisms. Even today, we don't have a complete understanding of all the factors involved in speciation. The most widely accepted explanation is that a new species is formed when part of a population becomes isolated from the rest and then, for whatever reasons, develops in a new direction.

The polar bear is an example of a species which fits this model very well. It's a relatively new species, having arisen less than 300,000 years ago—long after the first humans came on the scene. It probably evolved when a small population of grizzly bears at the northern edge of their range, amongst the glaciers of Siberia or Alaska, became isolated from the rest of the population. Over time, this northern group would have developed differently. For example, newborn grizzly bear cubs show natural variation in colour, from very pale brown to almost black. Pale-coloured cubs might have survived better in the snowy conditions, being able to creep up on prey without being so easily detected; white fur would eventually have conferred selective advantages and contributed to defining a new bear species.

Even though the polar bear outwardly looks very different from the brown bear, the genetic differences are not so great—confirming that the two species diverged only recently. Apart from fur colour, the polar bear differs from the brown bear in being larger, having smaller ears but bigger teeth, and having a digestive system better adapted to an entirely meat-based diet. DNA analysis shows the two bear species to be closely related, and several reports of hybridisation between polar bears and brown bears confirm this.

Polar bears are not the only white bears in the wild. In the wilderness of Canada's western coast, another type of white bear can sometimes be found. This is, paradoxically, the *black* bear—an entirely different species from the brown grizzly bear and the white polar bear. Widespread in Canada and the U.S., this bear—as its name suggests—is indeed black, but not always. On certain small islands in the temperate rainforest zone of British Colombia, it is sometimes actually white, so it resembles a polar bear. The white coloration of this black bear (known locally as the "ghost bear" or "spirit bear", for ecotouristic reasons) is caused not by albinism but by a recessive gene which finds expression in up to 10 percent of the bear population on Gribbell and Princess Royal Islands. The proportion is slightly less on the mainland and on other islands.[8]

It's not clear whether all these white-coated black bears are the result of natural selection or of genetic drift. If the variation did spread by natural selection, then possibly a group of bears at some time became isolated in an icy region where those with the palest fur survived best (as with polar bears). A later removal of a barrier to migration may have led to remixing of the two populations. But it's also possible that the white coloration is simply a chance variation which has been able to "live on" because the ghost bears manage just as well in the forest as their darker cousins do.

Killer whales

Just off shore from the ghost bears' islands, an interesting development is under way, one which may represent the first step towards the evolution of a new species. The killer whales, or orcas, in the waters around Vancouver Island are virtually a symbol of British Columbia and attract thousands of tourists every summer.

But the whales seen here are divided into two quite distinct populations. The so-called resident orcas eat mainly salmon and other fish. They live in large family groups of up to 30 individuals and are often acoustically very active: hydrophones pick up lively communication consisting of whistles and melodic calls. Members of the other population, known as "transients", live off other marine mammals such as seals, sea lions, and other cetaceans. They travel in small pods of only three to five individuals and—unlike the residents—are also commonly seen singly. They are very silent, only occasionally making soft contact calls. It makes sense for them not to "warn" their prey of their presence, as mammals have excellent hearing under water.

These two types of orcas differ not only in their behaviour. In terms of their appearance, they are superficially similar in their size, black-and-white coloration, and tall dorsal fins, but there are smaller distinctions if one looks closely. Slightly smaller than residents, transients have more triangular and pointed dorsal fins. Observations indicate that the two types of whales do not interact with each other, even though they live in the same waters; moreover, DNA analysis confirms that they do not mate. Within each type, there is very little genetic variation: in other words, they are inbred. But between the types there is considerable variation—more, in fact, than between Pacific orcas and Atlantic orcas. It's precisely these kinds of differences we expect to see in a species which is about to divide into two.[9] At present, all orcas still belong to the same species, even if some behave as if they didn't. If this situation continues for long enough time, an actual new species may yet evolve.

Mosquitos take the tube

Evolution can take place very quickly. The London Underground system is home to a special kind of mosquito, *Culex molestus*, which certainly hasn't had the benefit of millions, or even thousands, of years to adapt to its environment. The first stretches of the Underground were opened only in 1863; at some point since then, these mosquitoes—which normally live a typical insect life above ground—established themselves deep under the city streets. The tunnels of the Underground provide an excellent habitat for a mosquito, according to mosquito expert Katharine Byrne of the London Insitute of Zoology—a fairly constant temperature and humidity, no snow or frost, and few predators. Byrne studied the mosquitoes, finding that genetic differences have arisen even on different lines of the Underground: the Victoria, Bakerloo, and Central lines each have their own type of *C. molestus*!

Culex molestus looks identical to the above-ground mosquito *Culex pipiens*, a close relative, but its behaviour is very different. *C. pipiens* prefers to bite birds and hibernates in winter, whereas *C. molestus* attacks humans and is active year-round. Breeding experiments show that both types of mosquito can lay eggs and produce fertile offspring, but crosses between the two types are sterile.[10] Although this could be seen as support for the idea that they represent two separate species, scientists still do not agree on that point.

Surprise from the Galápagos

While Darwin was collecting animals and plants on the Galápagos Islands, dreaming of returning home to England, an unknown species of land iguana was living undisturbed and unnoticed near Wolf Volcano on the island of Isabela. Darwin never visited this volcano, so never saw this special iguana, which has a unique pink coloration. In fact, the iguana was not discovered until 1986, when some Galápagos National Park rangers reported having seen land iguanas living around the volcano; These iguanas looked pink rather than displaying the yellow and brown colours of the land iguanas the rangers knew from the other islands.

Typically for the Galápagos, the new land iguana turned out to be a separate species. Two land iguana species had previously been identified on the Galápagos, one being widely distributed throughout the islands and the other found on only one island. Comparisons between the DNA of the three species have shown that the new pink iguana is more different from the other two than they are from each other. This indicates that the pink form diverged from the other land iguanas first and that the two others split off more recently. Geneticists worked out in 2009 that the first split in the family tree took place about 5.7 million years ago, when some of the islands in the Galápagos group had not yet formed. So the newly described pink iguana is actually one the oldest inhabitants of the islands![11]

The discovery of this ancient species also underlines very neatly the observations Darwin made on the Galápagos, confirming something he recognised as he began to study so many different but closely related species: islands are fantastic "species factories".

CHAPTER 13

Evolution and religion

DARWIN'S THEORY OF evolution has changed our view of the world. In the same way that Copernicus and Galileo proved that Earth was not the centre of the universe, with everything else revolving around it, Darwin showed that man was simply one species amongst many others on Earth: we were a part of nature. This pill was not made any easier for his opponents to swallow by the fact that Darwin proposed a very simple mechanism for evolution: natural selection, which made superfluous the very idea of God the Creator.

Both evolution and natural selection met with strong resistance, especially from religious circles, and still do to this day. Paradoxically, opposition to the theory of evolution has not lessened despite the colossal amount of evidence in its favour which has been amassed in the past 150 years. In the United States especially, controversy over the teaching of evolution has even led to a number of lawsuits.

The Monkey Trial

The first trial in a U.S. court which saw evolution in the dock took place in 1925. The senate of the state of Tennessee had enacted legislation forbidding schools and universities from teaching any theory that denied the Biblical story of creation. The law emphasised in particular that it was prohibited to teach that mankind had evolved from "lower" animals. Oklahoma and Arkansas had similar laws on the statute books by the beginning of the 1920s, and there were attempts to ban the teaching of evolution in many other states too, although these did not succeed.

The American Civil Liberties Union (ACLU), newly founded at this time, saw an opportunity to challenge the anti-evolutionist state legislation on account of its religious basis. Central to their argument was the First Amendment to the U.S. Constitution, which guarantees religious freedom and separates church and state. The ACLU contended that any law either permitting or forbidding something on religious grounds would be contrary to the constitution. In order to test this in court, they needed someone willing to stand accused of teaching evolution in breach of the law. Accordingly, the ACLU placed advertisements in Tennessee newspapers, seeking citizens prepared to challenge the state legislation.

In the town of Dayton, Tennessee, a group of citizens associated with the ACLU managed to find a young high school teacher, John Scopes, who was happy to stand up and admit that, yes, he had taught the theory of evolution. Both this group and Scopes were interested in having the question tried in court, because they felt that the law hindered the advancement of science. Scopes (who was actually employed as a sports coach at the high school) could not recall whether, in his occasional lessons as a stand-in biology teacher, he had ever specifically made a connection between the evolution of men and apes. However, he was willing to be prosecuted if some pupils could be found to bear witness against him! They could indeed be found, so on July 10, 1925, one of the most bizarre trials in history began. Despite protests by the defence, the judge opened the trial every day with a prayer' moreover, the scene was set in the courtroom by a large banner hanging over the spectators' gallery and bearing the exhortation "Read your Bible".

Prosecuting authorities were represented by a legal team whose most prominent member was 65-year-old William Jennings Bryan, three times an unsuccessful presidential candidate. He was also a devout believer, which strongly affected the trial's outcome, especially when chief defence counsel Clarence Darrow called him as a witness in order to expose the Biblical point of view on a lengthy series of scientific questions. Bryan willingly played this role, even though his blind faith in the literal truth of the Bible made him look ridiculous in some eyes.

Here are some brief extracts from some of the more entertaining dialogues in the trial.[1]

Q: But when you read that Jonah swallowed the whale—or that the whale swallowed Jonah—excuse me please—how do you literally interpret that?

A: When I read that a big fish swallowed Jonah—it does not say whale.... That is my recollection of it. A big fish, and I believe it, and I believe in a God who can make a whale and can make a man and make both what He pleases.

Q: Now, you say, the big fish swallowed Jonah, and he there remained how long—three days—and then he spewed him upon the land. You believe that the big fish was made to swallow Jonah?

A: I am not prepared to say that; the Bible merely says it was done.

Q: You don't know whether it was the ordinary run of fish, or made for that purpose?

A: You may guess; you evolutionists guess...

Q: You are not prepared to say whether that fish was made especially to swallow a man or not?

A: The Bible doesn't say, so I am not prepared to say.

Q: But do you believe He made them—that He made such a fish and that it was big enough to swallow Jonah?

A: Yes, sir. Let me add: One miracle is just as easy to believe as another.

Q: Just as hard?

A: It is hard to believe for you, but easy for me. A miracle is a thing performed beyond what man can perform. When you get within the realm of miracles; and it is just as easy to believe the miracle of Jonah as any other miracle in the Bible.

Q: Perfectly easy to believe that Jonah swallowed the whale?

A: If the Bible said so; the Bible doesn't make as extreme statements as evolutionists do....

Thus the discussion bounced backwards and forwards in the courtroom. Darrow asked Bryan whether he truly believed that Joshua had made the sun stand still, as is written in the Old Testament; which animals he thought had made it onto Noah's Ark; whether Eve was made from Adam's rib; and whether it really made sense that the Earth was only 6,000 years old. Bryan readily answered all the questions.

The prosecution then called Howard Morgan, one of the school pupils, to the witness stand in order to hear what exactly had been taught in Scopes's lessons. Morgan was questioned first by prosecuting attorney General Stewart (who, incidentally, was not a military man—that was just his name).

Q: Did you study anything under Prof. Scopes?

A: Yes, sir.

Q: Did you study this book, General Science?

A: Yes, sir.

Q: Were you studying that book in April of this year, Howard?

A: Yes, sir.

Q: Did Prof. Scopes teach it to you?

A: Yes, sir.

Q: When did you complete the book?

A: Latter part of April.

Q: When was school out?

A: First or second of May.

Q: You studied it, then, up to a week or so before school was out?

A: Yes, sir.

Q: Now, you say you were studying this book in April; how did Prof. Scopes teach that book to you? I mean by that, did he ask you questions and you answered them, or did he give you lectures, or both? Just explain to the jury here now, these gentleman here in front of you, how he taught the books to you.

A: Well, sometimes he would ask us questions, and then he would lecture to us on different subjects in the book.

Q: Sometimes he asked you questions, and sometimes lectured to you on different subjects in the book?

A: Yes, sir.

Q: Did he ever undertake to teach you anything about evolution?

A: Yes, sir.

Q: Just state in your own words, Howard, what he taught you and when it was.

A: It was along about the 2nd of April.

Q: Of this year?

A: Yes, sir, of this year. He said that the Earth was once a hot molten mass, too hot for plant or animal life to exist upon it; in the sea, the Earth cooled off; there was a little germ of one cell organism formed; and this organism kept evolving until it got to be a pretty good-sized animal and then came on to be a land animal; and it kept on evolving, and from this was man.

Q: Let me repeat that; perhaps a little stronger than you. If I don't get it right, you correct me.

I ask you further, Howard, how did he classify man with reference to other animals; what did he say about them?

A: Well, the book and he both classified man along with cats and dogs, cows, horses, monkeys, lions, horses, and all that.

Q: What did he say they were?

A: Mammals.

Q: Classified them along with dogs, cats, horses, monkeys, and cows?

A: Yes, sir.

When Darrow cross-examined the witness for the defence, he also took up the question of classification:

Q: Let's see, your name is what?

A: Howard Morgan.

Q: Now, Howard, what do you mean by classify?

A: Well, it means classify these animals we mentioned, that men were just the same as them, in other words ...

Q: He didn't say a cat was the same as a man?

A: No, sir; he said man had a reasoning power; that these animals did not.

Q: There is some doubt about that, but that is what he said, is it? (Laughter in the courtroom.)

Despite Darrow's doughty efforts, Scopes was found guilty of teaching evolution in contravention of Tennessee's legislation. His fine of $100 was promptly paid by the Baltimore Sun newspaper. Bryan died of a heart attack five days after the conclusion of the trial.

Thus the first trial in a U.S. court in which the teaching of evolution and Christian beliefs were opposed to each other was lost by the proponents of evolution, with significant consequences for the teaching of science in American schools and universities over the following decades. One-hundred dollars was not a harsh punishment, yet this was still a landmark ruling: it encouraged other state legislatures to move in the same direction as Tennessee, Oklahoma, and Arkansas. Another development arising from this event was the concept of "creation science": an attempt to lend scientific credibility to the Biblical story of creation. It is still with us to this day.

Lawsuits continue

In the U.S. from the 1960s onwards, a series of court cases regarding the teaching of evolution were brought. In 1968, the ACLU again took the initiative by challenging another state legislature which had passed anti-evolution laws in the 1920s: Arkansas. This time, the case went to the U.S. Supreme Court, where the ACLU won convincingly. The unanimous verdict of the nine Supreme Court judges stated, "It is clear that fundamentalist sectarian conviction was and is the law's reason for existence"[2] and that it was therefore in violation of the Constitution.

However, the Arkansas opposition remained strong and in 1982 was back in court. School authorities had required that equal teaching time should be given to "creation science" as to Darwinist evolutionary theory. The court ruled that "creation science" was not science, but rather a religion, and should therefore not be brought into science lessons at all.

A very similar case was tried in Louisiana in 1986, where local authorities had passed a "creationism act" forbidding the teaching of evolution unless it was "balanced" by the teaching of "creation science". Once again, a court ruled that creationism was religion, not science, and that it was therefore unconstitutional to teach it in public schools.[3] The court found that, by advancing the religious belief that a supernatural being created humankind (a belief embraced by the term "creation science"), the act impermissibly endorsed a particular religious viewpoint. In addition, the court found that provision of a comprehensive science education is undermined when it is forbidden to teach evolution except when creation science is also taught.

But this was still only the beginning of a very long campaign. After these court rulings quashing the validity of "creation science" on constitutional grounds, opponents of evolution changed tactics and came up with a new idea, "intelligent design", as a rival model to the natural sciences.

Creationism and intelligent design

Creationism is a term for the opinion that the Biblical story of creation should be taken literally and that Earth (and everything on it) was created by a supernatural being. There are many degrees of creationism, from the most fundamental—which insists that Earth is only 6,000 years old and that all living creatures (and fossils) were created at the same time—to a more nuanced form allowing that Earth is very old and that not all organisms have been here since the beginning. The so-called "young Earth" creationists take the words of Genesis quite literally, maintaining that Earth—and life itself—was made in six days and that mankind was created at the same time as all other creatures. They think that fossils and all other evidence of evolution over the aeons are simply skilful forgeries.

Some of the more literal-minded creationists even have their own "Creation Museum" in Petersburg, Kentucky. Just as in any other natural history museum, visitors can admire life-like montages of animals and plants—but with the special twist that humans and dinosaurs appear together in the same scenes, even though science has determined that dinosaurs died out 65 million years ago (60 million years before the first humans walked on Earth). Permanent exhibits include the Garden of Eden and Noah's Ark as well as the Flood Room, where spectators can see sinners being engulfed, and swept away, by the waters.

After the teaching of "creation science" was declared unscientific and unconstitutional in the late 1980s, it was replaced by the concept of "intelligent design". The intelligent design movement distanced itself from the "young Earth" creationists by acknowledging that the Earth is old and that species can change, up to a point. Some proponents even accepted that humans and apes had common origins. Their main argument holds that there are many highly complex living organisms (as well as organs) which cannot have arisen through natural selection—because they would not have worked until fully evolved.

As a metaphor of such a complex system that only works when complete, the intelligent design movement has used the mouse trap. This consists of a spring, a clamp, a wooden base, and a trigger allowing the clamp to snap down onto the mouse. If any one of these parts is removed, the trap doesn't work. Similarly, they contend, many complex biological systems such as eyes or wings don't work as eyes or wings unless complete. Creationists argue that it is difficult to see how they can have arisen by means of an incremental evolutionary process, therefore they must have been designed by a conscious intelligence—just as William Paley argued in 1802. Modern adherents of intelligent design are usually careful to avoid mentioning "God" as the designer, at least in statements meant for the general public, but there seem to be few other candidates for the job of cosmic engineer.

A biologist could easily untangle the logical fallacy in this conclusion. A mouse trap may not work as a mouse trap until completely assembled, but all its component parts could function very well for other ends: without the trigger, the trap could make an excellent paper clip, while the trigger itself could be used as a fish hook. Similarly, the components of a complex biological system might easily have evolved separately for entirely different purposes. Feathers, for example, may have evolved originally to insulate the bodies of dinosaurs but now enable birds, their descendants, to fly.

Kitzmiller v. Dover Area School Board

In due course, intelligent design was put on trial in a U.S. court, just as creation science had been 20 years previously. In the little town of Dover, Pennsylvania, the school board had decided that pupils should learn about intelligent design and Darwinian evolution as equally plausible explanations of life on Earth. A group of parents in the school district brought the case, because they didn't want their children's science lessons to include either a creationist or an intelligent design version of the story of life. Again, the case was supported by the ACLU.

A central issue of the 2005 trial was whether any difference between creationism and intelligent design existed, as the intelligent design advocates argued. The question was crucial, as "creation science" had already been rejected as non-science by the U.S. Supreme Court. The case for the defence therefore rested on showing that intelligent design differed from "creation science" and was, by contrast, based on real science. Barbara Forrest, professor of philosophy at Southeastern Louisiana University and a key witness for the plaintiffs, had closely examined *Of Pandas and People*, the leading intelligent design school textbook. (The intelligent design lobby proposed using this book in Dover schools, in lieu of standard biology textbooks.) In a master stroke, Forrest presented a graph showing how, after the earlier trials of the 1980s condemning creationism, the word "creationism" had simply been removed from successive editions. At the same time, the words "intelligent design" took its place. Thus the contents of the books remained exactly the same: only the words "creation" and "creationism" had been removed.

Other expert prosecution witnesses both described what the scientific method consisted of (and how this differed from the intelligent design approach) and also explained some of the evidence for Darwinian evolution. Dr. Ken Miller of Brown University, a biologist and also a Catholic, delivered an analysis of weaknesses in the arguments for intelligent design; equally importantly, he also explained why it was possible to be a Christian believer and at the same time to be convinced of the theory of evolution: "The evolutionary theory is fully compatible with our different religious beliefs, but we also recognize that our religious beliefs are not scientific, that they are philosophical, theological, and deeply personal, and, as such, they don't belong in a science curriculum, and they certainly don't belong in a science textbook".[4]

Chief defence witness Dr. Michael Behe, professor of biochemistry at Lehigh University and a supporter of intelligent design was forced under pressure to admit that not a single scientific article supporting the idea of intelligent design had been published in a peer-reviewed journal.

In a crushing defeat for intelligent design, the judge ruled it had no scientific basis and was a purely religious construction. Intelligent design was dependent on a supernatural explanation, in defiance of one of the most basic principles of the natural sciences.

Evolution and creationism in Europe

Although all recent court cases in the U.S. have been won by the scientists rather than the creationists, the dispute there about the teaching of evolution is far from over. Apart from Turkey, no other industrialised country has a lower percentage of citizens who agree with the statement "Human beings, as we know them, developed from earlier species of animals". One-third of all adult Americans reject evolution completely, and only 14 percent say they completely agree that evolution exists.[5]

The situation is quite different in Europe, where the Nordic countries lie near the top of the table and up to 80 percent are convinced by evolution. However, in recent years creationism and intelligent design have made waves in Europe as well. In the 2000s, U.S.-based evangelical organisations such as "Answers in Genesis" funded branches in Europe. The curiously named "Truth in Science" campaign sent out free DVDs to every school in Britain, promoting the idea that mankind is the result of "intelligent design" rather than Darwinian evolution. Even a European education minister—Dutch Christian Democrat Maria van der Hoeven—was moved to declare that Darwin's theories were incomplete and should be supplemented by intelligent design. A Turkish propagandist known as Harun Yahya sent tens of thousands of unsolicited copies of his 700-page, illustrated book *The Atlas of Creation* to schools and universities all over Europe. The book denies evolution and declares all evidence in its favor to be false or misinterpreted.

The spread of creationist ideas in the education sector caused such concern that in 2007, the Council of Europe adopted a resolution entitled *The dangers of creationism in education*. The resolution observed that "The war on the theory of evolution and on its proponents most often originates in forms of religious extremism closely linked to extreme right-wing political movements" and urged that member states should "firmly oppose the teaching of creationism as a scientific discipline on an equal footing with the theory of evolution".[6]

But the struggle hasn't ended. The book "Creationism in Europe", edited by three scientists from Belgium and Denmark, concludes that anti-evolution is a growing problem in Europe. Charting the spread of creationism in Europe, the book found that creationism, creation science, intelligent design, and organised anti-evolutionism is a growing problem.[7] This is especially apparent in discussions of schools and their science curricula, but it's also increasingly noticeable on the Internet. Paradoxically, creationism and other anti-evolutionary ideas are gaining a foothold in more places at the same time that science is finding ever more proofs of evolution.

Darwin and faith

Darwin himself was not much troubled by religious questions. As a young man, he was a believer who took the Bible seriously, as he reported years later in his memoirs: "Whilst on board the *Beagle* I was quite orthodox, and I remember being heartily laughed at by several of the officers (though themselves orthodox) for quoting the Bible as an unanswerable authority on some point of morality."[8] But shortly after his return to England, his doubts had become stronger—so much so that he felt obliged to tell Emma of them before they were married. There was no dramatic rejection of Christianity as such, but gradually his faith faded: "Thus disbelief crept over me at a very slow rate, but was at last complete".[9]

Some historians believe that the death of his daughter, Annie, was the last straw, putting an end to Darwin's faltering faith. He certainly found it hard to reconcile belief in an almighty God with the suffering and torments he saw all around him. In a letter to the American botanist Asa Gray, a practising Christian and a colleague with whom Darwin regularly discussed questions of religion, he wrote: "An innocent & good man stands under tree & is killed by flash of lightning.

Do you believe (& I really shd like to hear) that God designedly killed this man? Many or most persons do believe this; I can't & don't".[10] To Asa Gray he also wrote about the *Ichneumonidae*, a group of parasitic wasps which lay their eggs inside the larvae of other insects: "There seems to me too much misery in the world. I cannot persuade myself that a beneficent & omnipotent God would have designedly created the Ichneumonidæ with the express intention of their feeding within the living bodies of caterpillars, or that a cat should play with mice".[11]

Darwin's final years

The last scientific project which Darwin undertook in his old age was very appropriate: a study of earthworms and how they transformed organic matter into soil. As always, his observations were detailed and precise, and his special talent for devising simple and effective experiments had not deserted him. To test the worms' sensitivity to vibration, he placed them in flowerpots on top of the piano in the living room, where he could observe how they would react to the piano being played.

In his late years, Darwin reflected on the impact he had on the world. He knew very well, even many years before writing *On the Origin of Species*, how groundbreaking his ideas were. "I have just finished my sketch of my species theory. If, as I believe that my theory is true & if it be accepted by even one competent judge, it will be a considerable step in science",[12] he confided to his wife in a letter in 1844.

It was indeed a considerable step in science—a step that changed forever the way we as humans understand the world, how we think life has evolved on it, and how our own species fits in. Yet in Darwin's typically modest view of himself, he didn't consider himself anything special. "I have no great quickness of apprehension or wit which is so remarkable in some clever men … my power to follow a long and purely abstract train of thought is very limited … my memory is extensive, yet hazy", he confessed in his memoirs. He concluded them with this humble statement: "With such moderate abilities as I possess, it is truly surprising that thus I should have influenced to a considerable extent the beliefs of scientific men on some important points."[13]

As his strength began to fail, Darwin was well aware that he was becoming old and feeble. The day after his 73rd birthday, he wrote in a letter: "I feel a very old man and my course is nearly run.[14] He was to complete his life's journey two months later. Darwin died on the April 19, 1882, in his bed at Down House, with Emma and several of his children by his side. His son Francis reported that he seemed to recognise the approach of death and that his final words were "I am not the least afraid to die".[15]

In stark contrast to Darwin's life, his burial was neither quiet nor private. Immediately following his death, a group of scientists and MPs petitioned for the nation's greatest scientist of the day to be interred in Westminster Abbey, near Isaac Newton. Charles Darwin's theory of the evolution of life had changed the world for all time; it felt right that his final resting place would be close to his country-man who had brought equally epoch-making ideas to his own generation. The ceremony was attended by dignitaries and leading figures from all sections of the Establishment, but also by his faithful servant Parslow and his cook Mrs Evans. Lyell had already passed away, but the remaining musketeers—Hooker, Wallace, and Huxley—were amongst the pallbearers.

Darwin had solved some of life's biggest questions: who are we, and where do we come from? These questions are so big that few would dare tackle them. But as he himself said: "Ignorance more frequently begets confidence than does knowledge: it is those who know little, and not those who know much, who so positively assert that this or that problem will never be solved by science".[16]

He knew much.

Notes to chapter 1

1. Darwin, Francis ed. 1887. *The life and letters of Charles Darwin, including an autobiographical chapter*. London: John Murray. Volume 1. Page 28. In John van Wyhe, ed. 2002- *The Complete Work of Charles Darwin Online* (http://darwin-online.org.uk)

2. Darwin, Francis ed. 1887. *The life and letters of Charles Darwin, including an autobiographical chapter*. London: John Murray. Volume 1. Page 27. In John van Wyhe, ed. 2002- *The Complete Work of Charles Darwin Online* (http://darwin-online.org.uk)

3. Darwin, Francis ed. 1887. *The life and letters of Charles Darwin, including an autobiographical chapter*. London: John Murray. Volume 1. Page 44. In John van Wyhe, ed. 2002- *The Complete Work of Charles Darwin Online* (http://darwin-online.org.uk)

4. William Paley. 1802. *Natural Theology*. Page 1

5. Darwin, Francis ed. 1887. *The life and letters of Charles Darwin, including an autobiographical chapter*. London: John Murray. Volume 1. Page 59. In John van Wyhe, ed. 2002- *The Complete Work of Charles Darwin Online* (http://darwin-online.org.uk)

6. Darwin, Francis ed. 1887. *The life and letters of Charles Darwin, including an autobiographical chapter*. London: John Murray. Volume 1. Page 52. In John van Wyhe, ed. 2002- *The Complete Work of Charles Darwin Online* (http://darwin-online.org.uk)

7. Darwin Correspondence Database, http://www.darwinproject. ac.uk/entry-789 accessed on Fri Jul 31 2015. Correspondence of Charles Darwin: 1844-1846 (vol-3). Burkhardt, F., and Smith, S. Cambridge University Press, 1988. Reproduced by permission from Cambridge University Press.

8. Darwin Correspondence Database, http://www.darwinproject. ac.uk/entry-729 accessed on Fri Jul 31 2015. Correspondence of Charles Darwin: 1844-1846 (vol-3). Burkhardt, F., and Smith, S. Cambridge University Press, 1988. Reproduced by permission from Cambridge University Press.

9. Darwin, Francis ed. 1887. *The life and letters of Charles Darwin, including an autobiographical chapter.* London: John Murray. Volume 1. Page 38. In John van Wyhe, ed. 2002- *The Complete Work of Charles Darwin Online* (http://darwin-online.org.uk)

10. Ibid.

Notes to chapter 2

1. Darwin, C.R. 1958. *The autobiography of Charles Darwin 1809-1882. With the original omissions restored. Edited and with appendix and notes by his grand-daughter Nora Barlow.* London: Collins. Page 57. In John van Wyhe, ed. 2002- *The Complete Work of Charles Darwin Online* (http://darwin-online.org.uk)

2. Darwin Correspondence Database, https://www.darwinproject. ac.uk/entry-42 accessed on Sun Jul 26 2015. The Correspondence of Charles Darwin: 1821-1836 (vol-1). Burkhardt, F., and Smith,

S. Cambridge University Press, 1985. Reproduced by permission from Cambridge University Press.

3. Darwin, Francis ed. 1887. *The life and letters of Charles Darwin, including an autobiographical chapter.* London: John Murray. Volume 1. Page 221. In John van Wyhe, ed. 2002- *The Complete Work of Charles Darwin Online* (http://darwin-online.org.uk)

4. Darwin, Francis ed. 1887. *The life and letters of Charles Darwin, including an autobiographical chapter.* London: John Murray. Volume 1. Page 222. In John van Wyhe, ed. 2002- *The Complete Work of Charles Darwin Online* (http://darwin-online.org.uk)

5. Darwin, Francis ed. 1887. *The life and letters of Charles Darwin, including an autobiographical chapter.* London: John Murray. Volume 1. Page 72. In John van Wyhe, ed. 2002- *The Complete Work of Charles Darwin Online* (http://darwin-online.org.uk)

6. Darwin, C.R. 1839. *Narrative of the surveying voyages of His Majesty's Ships Adventure and Beagle between the years 1826 and 1836, describing their examination of the southern shores of South America, and the Beagle's circumnavigation of the globe. Journal and remarks. 1832–1836.* London: Henry Colburn. In John van Wyhe, ed. 2002- *The Complete Work of Charles Darwin Online* (http://darwin-online.org.uk)

7. Darwin, Francis ed. 1887. *The life and letters of Charles Darwin, including an autobiographical chapter.* London: John Murray. Volume 1. Page 62. In John van Wyhe, ed. 2002- *The Complete Work of Charles Darwin Online* (http://darwin-online.org.uk)

8. Darwin, C.R. 1839. *Narrative of the surveying voyages of His Majesty's Ships Adventure and Beagle between the years 1826 and 1836, describing their examination of the southern shores of South America, and the Beagle's circumnavigation of the globe. Journal and remarks. 1832–1836.* London: Henry Colburn. Page 406. In John van Wyhe, ed. 2002- *The Complete Work of Charles Darwin Online* (http://darwin-online.org.uk)

9. Darwin, C.R. 1839. *Narrative of the surveying voyages of His Majesty's Ships Adventure and Beagle between the years 1826 and 1836, describing their examination of the southern shores of South America, and the Beagle's circumnavigation of the globe. Journal and remarks. 1832–1836.* London: Henry Colburn. Page 379. In John van Wyhe, ed. 2002- *The Complete Work of Charles Darwin Online* (http://darwin-online.org.uk)

10. FitzRoy, R. 1839. *Narrative of the surveying voyages of His Majesty's Ships Adventure and Beagle between the years 1826 and 1836, describing their examination of the southern shores of South America, and the Beagle's circumnavigation of the globe. Proceedings of the second expedition, 1831–36, under the command of Captain Robert FitzRoy, R.N.* London: Henry Colburn. Page 658. In John van Wyhe, ed. 2002- *The Complete Work of Charles Darwin Online* (http://darwin-online.org.uk)

11. Ibid.

12. Darwin Correspondence Database, https://www.darwinproject.ac.uk/entry-542 accessed on Sun Jul 26 2015. The Correspondence of Charles Darwin: 1837-1843 (vol-2). Burkhardt, F., and Smith, S. Cambridge University Press, 1987. Reproduced by permission from Cambridge University Press.

13. Alvarez, L.W., Alvarez, W., Asaro, F., and Michel, H.V. 1980. Extraterrestrial cause for the Cretaceous–Tertiary extinction. *Science* 208(4448): pages 1095–1108.

14. Alvarez, W. 1997. *T. rex and the Crater of Doom*. Princeton University Press.

15. Darwin Correspondence Database, https://www.darwinproject. ac.uk/entry-602 accessed on Sun Jul 26 2015. The Correspondence of Charles Darwin: 1837-1843 (vol-2). Burkhardt, F., and Smith, S. Cambridge University Press, 1987. Reproduced by permission from Cambridge University Press.

16. Rosing, M., Bird, D.K., Sleep, N.H., Glassley, W., and Albarède, F. 2006. The rise of continents: An essay on the geologic consequences of photosynthesis. *Palaeogeography, Palaeoclimatology, Palaeoecology*, no. 232, pages 99–113.

Notes to chapter 3

1. Darwin Correspondence Database, https://www.darwinproject. ac.uk/entry-154 accessed on Sun Jul 26 2015. The Correspondence of Charles Darwin: 1821-1836 (vol-1). Burkhardt, F., and Smith, S. Cambridge University Press, 1985.

2. Darwin Correspondence Database, https://www.darwinproject. ac.uk/entry-164 accessed on Sun Jul 26 2015. The Correspondence of Charles Darwin: 1821-1836 (vol-1). Burkhardt, F., and Smith, S. Cambridge University Press, 1985. Reproduced by permission from Cambridge University Press.

3. Darwin Correspondence Database, https://www.darwinproject.
ac.uk/entry-180 accessed on Sun Jul 26 2015. The Correspondence
of Charles Darwin: 1821-1836 (vol-1). Burkhardt, F., and Smith,
S. Cambridge University Press, 1985. Reproduced by permission
from Cambridge University Press.

4. Darwin Correspondence Database, https://www.darwinproject.
ac.uk/entry-206 accessed on Sun Jul 26 2015. The Correspondence
of Charles Darwin: 1821-1836 (vol-1). Burkhardt, F., and Smith,
S. Cambridge University Press, 1985. Reproduced by permission
from Cambridge University Press.

5. Darwin Correspondence Database, https://www.darwinproject.
ac.uk/entry-192 accessed on Sun Jul 26 2015. The Correspondence
of Charles Darwin: 1821-1836 (vol-1). Burkhardt, F., and Smith,
S. Cambridge University Press, 1985. Reproduced by permission
from Cambridge University Press.

6. Keynes, R.D. ed. 2001. *Charles Darwin's Beagle Diary*. Cambridge:
Cambridge University Press. In John van Wyhe, ed. 2002- *The
Complete Work of Charles Darwin Online* (http://darwin-online.
org.uk)

7. Keynes, R.D. ed. 2001. *Charles Darwin's Beagle Diary*. Cambridge:
Cambridge University Press. In John van Wyhe, ed. 2002- *The
Complete Work of Charles Darwin Online* (http://darwin-online.
org.uk)

8. Darwin Correspondence Database, https://www.darwinproject.
ac.uk/entry-192 accessed on Sun Jul 26 2015. The Correspondence
of Charles Darwin: 1821-1836 (vol-1). Burkhardt, F., and Smith,

S. Cambridge University Press, 1985. Reproduced by permission from Cambridge University Press.

9. Darwin Correspondence Database, https://www.darwinproject. ac.uk/entry-213 accessed on Sun Jul 26 2015. The Correspondence of Charles Darwin: 1821-1836 (vol-1). Burkhardt, F., and Smith, S. Cambridge University Press, 1985.

10. Darwin Correspondence Database, https://www.darwinproject. ac.uk/entry-288 accessed on Sun Jul 26 2015. The Correspondence of Charles Darwin: 1821-1836 (vol-1). Burkhardt, F., and Smith, S. Cambridge University Press, 1985. Reproduced by permission from Cambridge University Press.

11. Owen, Richard. *The Life of Richard Owen by His Grandson.* 2 vols. London: 1894.

12. Darwin, C. R. 1839. *Narrative of the surveying voyages of His Majesty's Ships Adventure and Beagle between the years 1826 and 1836, describing their examination of the southern shores of South America, and the Beagle's circumnavigation of the globe.* Journal and remarks. 1832–1836. London: Henry Colburn. In John van Wyhe, ed. 2002- *The Complete Work of Charles Darwin Online* (http://darwin-online.org.uk)

13. *The Zoology of the Voyage of H.M.S. Beagle, under the Command of Captain FitzRoy, R.N., during the Years 1832 to 1836.* Published with the approval of the Lords Commissioners of Her Majesty's Treasury. Edited and superintended by Charles Darwin, ESQ. M.A. F.R.S. Sec. G.S. Naturalist to the expedition. Part I. Fossil Mammalia: By Richard Owen, ESQ. F.R.S. Professor of

Anatomy and Physiology to The Royal College of Surgeons in London; Corresponding Member of The Institute of France, etc. etc. 1839–1843. In John van Wyhe, ed. 2002- *The Complete Work of Charles Darwin Online* (http://darwin-online.org.uk)

14. Ibid.

15. Keynes, R. D. ed. 2001. *Charles Darwin's Beagle Diary.* Cambridge: Cambridge University Press.(4–7 October 1833). In John van Wyhe, ed. 2002- *The Complete Work of Charles Darwin Online* (http://darwin-online.org.uk)

16. *The Zoology of the Voyage of H.M.S. Beagle, under the Command of Captain FitzRoy, R.N., during the Years 1832 to 1836.* Published with the approval of the Lords Commissioners of Her Majesty's Treasury. Edited and superintended by Charles Darwin, ESQ. M.A. F.R.S. SEC. G.S. Naturalist to the expedition. Part I. Fossil Mammalia: By Richard Owen, ESQ. F.R.S. Professor of Anatomy and Physiology to The Royal College of Surgeons In London; Corresponding Member of The Institute of France, etc. etc. 1839–1843. In John van Wyhe, ed. 2002- *The Complete Work of Charles Darwin Online* (http://darwin-online.org.uk)

17. Ibid.

18. Ibid.

19. Ibid.

20. Darwin, C. 1859. *On the Origin of Species by Means of Natural Selection, or the Preservation of Favoured Races in the Struggle for Life.*

London: John Murray. In John van Wyhe, ed. 2002- *The Complete Work of Charles Darwin Online* (http://darwin-online.org.uk)

21. Prideaux, G.J., Roberts, R.G., Megirian D., Westaway, K.E., Hellstrom, J.C., et al. 2007. Mammalian responses to Pleistocene climate change in southeastern Australia. *Geology* 35:1, pp. 33–36.

Notes to chapter 4

1. Darwin Correspondence Database, https://www.darwinproject.ac.uk/entry-215 accessed on Mon Jul 27 2015. The Correspondence of Charles Darwin: 1821-1836 (vol-1). Burkhardt, F., and Smith, S. Cambridge University Press, 1985. Reproduced by permission from Cambridge University Press.

2. Darwin, C. R. 1839. *Narrative of the surveying voyages of His Majesty's Ships Adventure and Beagle between the years 1826 and 1836, describing their examination of the southern shores of South America, and the Beagle's circumnavigation of the globe. Journal and remarks. 1832–1836.* London: Henry Colburn. In John van Wyhe, ed. 2002- *The Complete Work of Charles Darwin Online* (http://darwin-online.org.uk)

3. Keynes, Richard D. ed. 2001. *Charles Darwin's Beagle Diary.* Cambridge: Cambridge University Press. Page 212. In John van Wyhe, ed. 2002- *The Complete Work of Charles Darwin Online* (http://darwin-online.org.uk)

4. Darwin Correspondence Database, https://www.darwinproject.ac.uk/entry-282 accessed on Mon Jul 27 2015. The Correspondence

of Charles Darwin: 1821-1836 (vol-1). Burkhardt, F., and Smith, S. Cambridge University Press, 1985.

5. Ibid.

6. Darwin, C. R. 1839. *Narrative of the surveying voyages of His Majesty's Ships Adventure and Beagle between the years 1826 and 1836, describing their examination of the southern shores of South America, and the Beagle's circumnavigation of the globe. Journal and remarks. 1832–1836.* London: Henry Colburn. Page 454. In John van Wyhe, ed. 2002- *The Complete Work of Charles Darwin Online* (http://darwin-online.org.uk)

7. Darwin, C. R. 1839. *Narrative of the surveying voyages of His Majesty's Ships Adventure and Beagle between the years 1826 and 1836, describing their examination of the southern shores of South America, and the Beagle's circumnavigation of the globe. Journal and remarks. 1832-1836.* London: Henry Colburn. Page 468. In John van Wyhe, ed. 2002- *The Complete Work of Charles Darwin Online* (http://darwin-online.org.uk)

8. Keynes, Richard D. ed. 2001. *Charles Darwin's Beagle Diary.* Cambridge: Cambridge University Press. Page258. In John van Wyhe, ed. 2002- *The Complete Work of Charles Darwin Online* (http://darwin-online.org.uk)

9. Charles Darwin's Beagle animal notes (1832-33). Cambridge University Library—DAR29:1. Page 22. Transcribed by Richard Darwin Keynes. In John van Wyhe, ed. 2002- *The Complete Work of Charles Darwin Online* (http://darwin-online.org.uk)

10. Keynes, Richard D. ed. 2000. *Charles Darwin's zoology notes & specimen lists from H.M.S. Beagle.* Cambridge: Cambridge University Press. Page237. In John van Wyhe, ed. 2002- *The Complete Work of Charles Darwin Online* (http://darwin-online.org.uk)

11. Keynes, Richard D. ed. 2000. *Charles Darwin's zoology notes & specimen lists from H.M.S. Beagle.* Cambridge: Cambridge University Press. Page328. In John van Wyhe, ed. 2002- *The Complete Work of Charles Darwin Online* (http://darwin-online.org.uk)

12. Barlow, Nora ed. 1963. Darwin's ornithological notes. *Bulletin of the British Museum (Natural History).* Historical Series Volume 2, Number 7, pages 201–278. With introduction, notes and appendix by the editor. Page 262. Reproduced by permission of the Trustees of the Natural History Museum, London. In John van Wyhe, ed. 2002- *The Complete Work of Charles Darwin Online* (http://darwin-online.org.uk)

13. Lyell, Charles. 1853. *Principles of geology, being an attempt to explain the former changes of the Earth's surface, by reference to causes now in operation*, Volume 1. London: John Murray. Page 667.

14. Darwin, C.R. *Notebook B: [Transmutation of species (1837-1838)].* Cambridge University Library—DAR121. Page 16. Transcribed by Kees Rookmaaker. In John van Wyhe, ed. 2002- *The Complete Work of Charles Darwin Online* (http://darwin-online.org.uk)

15. Millien, V. 2006. Morphological evolution is accelerated among island mammals. *PLoS Biology* 4:e 321.

16. Roth L.V. 1992. Inferences from allometry and fossils: Dwarfing of elephants on islands. *Oxford Surveys in Evolutionary Biology.* Pages 259–288.

17. Burness, Gary P., Diamond, J., and Flannery, T. 2001. Dinosaurs, dragons, and dwarfs: The evolution of maximal body size. *Proceedings of the National Academy of Sciences U S A.* 98:25:14518–23.

18. Myers N., Mittermeier R.A., Mittermeier C.G., Fonseca G.A.B., and Kent J. 2000. Biodiversity hotspots for conservation priorities. *Nature.* 403:853–858.

19. Darwin, C.R. *Notebook B: [Transmutation of species (1837-1838)].* Cambridge University Library–DAR121. Page 15. Transcribed by Kees Rookmaaker. In John van Wyhe, ed. 2002- *The Complete Work of Charles Darwin Online* (http://darwin-online.org.uk)

20. James Marchant. 1916. *Alfred Russel Wallace: Letters and Reminiscences.* New York: Harper & Brothers. Letter to Bates in 1858.

21. Darwin Correspondence Database, https://www.darwin-project.ac.uk/entry-1669 accessed on Mon Jul 27 2015. The Correspondence of Charles Darwin: 1851-1855 (vol-5). Burkhardt, F., and Smith, S. Cambridge University Press, 1990.

22. Darwin Correspondence Database, https://www.darwin-project.ac.uk/entry-1707 accessed on Mon Jul 27 2015. The Correspondence of Charles Darwin: 1851-1855 (vol-5). Burkhardt, F., and Smith, S. Cambridge University Press, 1990.

23. Darwin Correspondence Database, https://www.darwin-project.ac.uk/entry-1669 accessed on Mon Jul 27 2015. The Correspondence of Charles Darwin: 1851-1855 (vol-5). Burkhardt, F., and Smith, S. Cambridge University Press, 1990.

Notes to chapter 5

1. Darwin Correspondence Database, https://www.darwinproject.ac.uk/entry-308 accessed on Tue Jul 28 2015. The Correspondence of Charles Darwin: 1821-1836 (vol-1). Burkhardt, F., and Smith, S. Cambridge University Press, 1985.

2. Darwin Correspondence Database, https://www.darwinproject.ac.uk/entry-317 accessed on Tue Jul 28 2015. The Correspondence of Charles Darwin: 1821-1836 (vol-1). Burkhardt, F., and Smith, S. Cambridge University Press, 1985.

3. Sulloway, F.J. 1982. The *Beagle* collections of Darwin's finches (*Geospizinae*). *Bulletin of the British Museum (Natural History) Historical Series* 43:2, pages 49–94. In John van Wyhe, ed. 2002- *The Complete Work of Charles Darwin Online* (http://darwin-online.org.uk)

4. Darwin, C.R. 1839. *Narrative of the surveying voyages of His Majesty's Ships Adventure and Beagle between the years 1826 and 1836, describing their examination of the southern shores of South America, and the Beagle's circumnavigation of the globe. Journal and remarks. 1832–1836.* London: Henry Colburn. In John van Wyhe, ed. 2002- *The Complete Work of Charles Darwin Online* (http://darwin-online.org.uk)

5. Darwin, C.R. 1845. *Journal of researches into the natural history and geology of the countries visited during the voyage of H.M.S. Beagle round the world, under the Command of Capt. FitzRoy, R.N.* Second edition. London: John Murray. In John van Wyhe, ed. 2002- *The Complete Work of Charles Darwin Online* (http://darwin-online.org.uk)

6. Roca, A.L., Georgiadis, N., Pecon-Slattery, J., and O'Brien, S.J. 2001. Genetic Evidence for Two Species of Elephant in Africa. *Science* 293 (5534), pages 1473–1477. [DOI: 10.1126/science.1059936].

7. Beale, Thomas. 1839. *The natural history of the sperm whale.* London: Van Voorst.

8. Mayr, Ernst. 1942. *Systematics and the origin of species from the viewpoint of a zoologist.* Cambridge: Harvard University Press.

9. Darwin Correspondence Database, https://www.darwinproject.ac.uk/entry-947 accessed on Tue Jul 28 2015. The Correspondence of Charles Darwin: 1844-1846 (vol-3). Burkhardt, F., and Smith, S. Cambridge University Press, 1988. Reproduced by permission from Cambridge University Press.

10. Darwin Correspondence Database, https://www.darwinproject.ac.uk/entry-1339 accessed on Tue Jul 28 2015. The Correspondence of Charles Darwin: 1844-1846 (vol-3). Burkhardt, F., and Smith, S. Cambridge University Press, 1988. Reproduced by permission from Cambridge University Press.

11. Darwin Correspondence Database, https://www.darwinproject.ac.uk/entry-424 accessed on Tue Jul 28 2015. The Correspondence of Charles Darwin: 1837-1843 (vol-2). Burkhardt, F., and Smith,

S. Cambridge University Press, 1987. Reproduced by permission from Cambridge University Press.

Notes to chapter 6

1. Darwin, C.R. 1958. *The autobiography of Charles Darwin 1809–1882. With the original omissions restored. Edited and with appendix and notes by his grand-daughter Nora Barlow.* London: Collins. Page 232. In John van Wyhe, ed. 2002- *The Complete Work of Charles Darwin Online* (http://darwin-online.org.uk)

2. Darwin, C.R. 1958. *The autobiography of Charles Darwin 1809–1882. With the original omissions restored. Edited and with appendix and notes by his grand-daughter Nora Barlow.* London: Collins. Page 234. In John van Wyhe, ed. 2002- *The Complete Work of Charles Darwin Online* (http://darwin-online.org.uk)

3. Darwin, C.R. 1958. *The autobiography of Charles Darwin 1809–1882. With the original omissions restored. Edited and with appendix and notes by his grand-daughter Nora Barlow.* London: Collins. Page 95. In John van Wyhe, ed. 2002- *The Complete Work of Charles Darwin Online* (http://darwin-online.org.uk)

4. Litchfield, H.E. ed. 1915. *Emma Darwin, A century of family letters, 1792–1896.* Volume 2. London: John Murray. In John van Wyhe, ed. 2002- *The Complete Work of Charles Darwin Online* (http://darwin-online.org.uk)

5. Malthus, Thomas. 1798. *An Essay on the Principle of Population, as it Affects the Future Improvement of Society with Remarks on*

the Speculations of Mr. Godwin, M. Condorcet, and Other Writers. London: Printed for J. Johnson, in St. Paul's Church-Yard.

6. Emslie, Steven D. and Patterson, William P. 2007. Abrupt recent shift in δ^{13}C and δ^{15}N values in Adélie penguin eggshell in Antarctica. *Proceedings of the National Academy of Sciences U S A* 104(28):11666–11669.

7. Darwin Correspondence Database, https://www.darwinproject. ac.uk/entry-2101 accessed on Tue Jul 28 2015. The Correspondence of Charles Darwin: 1856-1857 (vol-6). Burkhardt, F., and Smith, S. Cambridge University Press, 1990. Reproduced by permission from Cambridge University Press.

8. Ibid.

9. Darwin Correspondence Database, https://www.darwinproject. ac.uk/entry-465 accessed on Tue Jul 28 2015. The Correspondence of Charles Darwin: 1837-1843 (vol-2). Burkhardt, F., and Smith, S. Cambridge University Press, 1987. Reproduced by permission from Cambridge University Press.

Notes to chapter 7

1. Darwin, C.R. Notebook B: *[Transmutation of species (1837– 1838)]*. Cambridge University Library—DAR121. Page 229. Transcribed by Kees Rookmaaker. In John van Wyhe, ed. 2002- *The Complete Work of Charles Darwin Online* (http://darwin-online.org.uk)

2. Darwin, C.R. *Notebook B: [Transmutation of species (1837–1838)]*. Cambridge University Library—DAR121. Transcribed by Kees Rookmaaker. In John van Wyhe, ed. 2002- *The Complete Work of Charles Darwin Online* (http://darwin-online.org.uk)

3. Darwin, C.R. *Notebook B: [Transmutation of species (1837–1838)]*. Cambridge University Library—DAR121. Page 21. Transcribed by Kees Rookmaaker. In John van Wyhe, ed. 2002- *The Complete Work of Charles Darwin Online* (http://darwin-online.org.uk)

4. Darwin, C.R. *Notebook B: [Transmutation of species (1837–1838)]*. Cambridge University Library—DAR121. Page 25. Transcribed by Kees Rookmaaker. In John van Wyhe, ed. 2002- *The Complete Work of Charles Darwin Online* (http://darwin-online.org.uk)

5. Kristensen, M., Knorr, M., Rasmussen, A.-M., Jespersen, J.B. 2006. Survey of permethrin and malathion resistance in human head lice populations in Denmark. *Journal of Medical Entomology*. 43(3):533–8.

6. Enattah, N.S., Sahi, T., Savilahti, E., Terwilliger, J.D., Peltonen, et al. 2002. Identification of a variant associated with adult-type hypolactasia. *Nature Genetics* 30(2):233–237.

7. Tishkoff, S.A. et al. 2007. Convergent adaptation of human lactase persistence in Africa and Europe. *Nature Genetics* **39(1):**31–40.

8. Kettlewell, H.B.D. 1955. Selection experiments on industrial melanism in the Lepidoptera. *Heredity* 9:323–342. Kettlewell, H.B.D. 1956. Further selection experiments on industrial melanism in the Lepidoptera. *Heredity* 10:287–301.

9. Majerus, M.E.N. 1998. *Melanism: Evolution in Action*. Oxford: Oxford University Press.

10. Darwin, C.R. 1845. *Journal of researches into the natural history and geology of the countries visited during the voyage of H.M.S. Beagle round the world, under the Command of Capt. FitzRoy, R.N.* Second edition. London: John Murray. In John van Wyhe, ed. 2002- *The Complete Work of Charles Darwin Online* (http://darwin-online.org.uk)

11. Darwin Correspondence Database, http://www.darwinproject.ac.uk/entry-761 accessed on Wed Jul 29 2015. The Correspondence of Charles Darwin: 1844-1846 (vol-3). Burkhardt, F., and Smith, S. Cambridge University Press, 1988. Reproduced by permission from Cambridge University Press.

12. Darwin, C.R. *Shot [Notes on shooting]*. Cambridge University Library—DAR91.1. Transcribed and edited by Kees Rookmaaker 11.2008. In John van Wyhe, ed. 2002- *The Complete Work of Charles Darwin Online* (http://darwin-online.org.uk)

13. Darwin Correspondence Database, http://www.darwinproject.ac.uk/entry-814 accessed on Wed Jul 29 2015. The Correspondence of Charles Darwin: 1844-1846 (vol-3). Burkhardt, F., and Smith, S. Cambridge University Press, 1988. Reproduced by permission from Cambridge University Press.

14. Darwin Correspondence Database, http://www.darwinproject.ac.uk/entry-729 accessed on Wed Jul 29 2015. The Correspondence of Charles Darwin: 1844-1846 (vol-3). Burkhardt, F., and Smith, S. Cambridge University Press, 1988. Reproduced by permission from Cambridge University Press.

15. Darwin Correspondence Database, http://www.darwinproject. ac.uk/entry-734 accessed on Wed Jul 29 2015. The Correspondence of Charles Darwin: 1844-1846 (vol-3). Burkhardt, F., and Smith, S. Cambridge University Press, 1988. Reproduced by permission from Cambridge University Press.

16. Darwin Correspondence Database, http://www.darwinproject. ac.uk/entry-793 accessed on Wed Jul 29 2015. The Correspondence of Charles Darwin: 1844-1846 (vol-3). Burkhardt, F., and Smith, S. Cambridge University Press, 1988. Reproduced by permission from Cambridge University Press.

17. Darwin Correspondence Database, http://www.darwinproject. ac.uk/entry-828 accessed on Wed Jul 29 2015. The Correspondence of Charles Darwin: 1844-1846 (vol-3). Burkhardt, F., and Smith, S. Cambridge University Press, 1988. Reproduced by permission from Cambridge University Press.

18. Darwin Correspondence Database, http://www.darwinproject. ac.uk/entry-1174 accessed on Sat Aug 8 2015. The Correspondence of Charles Darwin: 1847-1850 (vol-4). Burkhardt, F., and Smith, S. Cambridge University Press, 1989. Reproduced by permission from Cambridge University Press.

Notes to chapter 8

1. Darwin Correspondence Database, http://www.darwinproject. ac.uk/entry-1408 accessed on Fri Jul 31 2015. The Correspondence of Charles Darwin: 1851-1855 (vol-5). Burkhardt, F., and Smith, S. Cambridge University Press, 1990. Reproduced by permission from Cambridge University Press.

2. Darwin Correspondence Database, http://www.darwinproject. ac.uk/entry-1425 accessed on Fri Jul 31 2015. The Correspondence of Charles Darwin: 1851-1855 (vol-5). Burkhardt, F., and Smith, S. Cambridge University Press, 1990. Reproduced by permission from Cambridge University Press.

3. Darwin Correspondence Database, http://www.darwinproject. ac.uk/entry-1174 accessed on Fri Jul 31 2015. The Correspondence of Charles Darwin: 1847-1850 (vol-4). Burkhardt, F., and Smith, S. Cambridge University Press, 1989. Reproduced by permission from Cambridge University Press.

4. Darwin Correspondence Database, http://www.darwinproject. ac.uk/entry-1651 accessed on Fri Jul 31 2015. The Correspondence of Charles Darwin: 1851-1855 (vol-5). Burkhardt, F., and Smith, S. Cambridge University Press, 1990. Reproduced by permission from Cambridge University Press.

5. Darwin Correspondence Database, http://www.darwinproject. ac.uk/entry-586 accessed on Fri Jul 31 2015. The Correspondence of Charles Darwin: 1837-1843 (vol-2). Burkhardt, F., and Smith, S. Cambridge University Press, 1987. Reproduced by permission from Cambridge University Press.

6. Darwin Correspondence Database, http://www.darwinproject. ac.uk/entry-1862 accessed on Fri Jul 31 2015. The Correspondence of Charles Darwin: 1856-1857 (vol-6). Burkhardt, F., and Smith, S. Cambridge University Press, 1990. Reproduced by permission from Cambridge University Press.

7. Darwin Correspondence Database, http://www.darwinproject. ac.uk/entry-1866 accessed on Fri Jul 31 2015. The Correspondence of Charles Darwin: 1856-1857 (vol-6). Burkhardt, F., and Smith, S. Cambridge University Press, 1990. Reproduced by permission from Cambridge University Press.

8. Wallace, Alfred Russel. 1855. On the law which has regulated the introduction of new species. *Annals and Magazine of Natural History (Ser. 2)* 16(93):184–196.

9. Darwin Correspondence Database, http://www.darwinproject. ac.uk/entry-2086 accessed on Fri Jul 31 2015. The Correspondence of Charles Darwin: 1856-1857 (vol-6). Burkhardt, F., and Smith, S. Cambridge University Press, 1990.

10. Darwin Correspondence Database, http://www.darwinproject. ac.uk/entry-2285 accessed on Fri Jul 31 2015. The Correspondence of Charles Darwin: 1858-1859 (vol-7). Burkhardt, F., and Smith, S. Cambridge University Press, 1992. Reproduced by permission from Cambridge University Press.

11. Darwin Correspondence Database, http://www.darwinproject. ac.uk/entry-2294 accessed on Fri Jul 31 2015. The Correspondence of Charles Darwin: 1858-1859 (vol-7). Burkhardt, F., and Smith, S. Cambridge University Press, 1992. Reproduced by permission from Cambridge University Press.

12. Wallace, Alfred Russel. 1905. *My Life: A Record of Events and Opinions.* London: Chapman & Hall.

13. Presidential address, *Proceedings of the Linnean Society of London*. 24 May 1859.

14. Darwin, C.R. 1871. *The descent of man, and selection in relation to sex*. First edition. London: John Murray. In John van Wyhe, ed. 2002- *The Complete Work of Charles Darwin Online* (http://darwin-online.org.uk)

15. Le Boeuf, B.J. and Mesnick, S. 1991. Sexual behavior of male northern elephant seals. 1: Lethal injuries to adult females. *Behaviour* 116(1):143–162.

16. Darwin, C.R. 1871. *The descent of man, and selection in relation to sex*. First edition. London: John Murray. In John van Wyhe, ed. 2002- *The Complete Work of Charles Darwin Online* (http://darwin-online.org.uk)

17. Jukema, J., Piersma. T. 2006. Permanent female mimics in a lekking shorebird. *Biology Letters* 2(2):161–164. DOI: 10.1098/rsbl.2005.0416.

18. Chu, K.C. 1988. Dive times and ventilation patterns of singing humpback whales (*Megaptera novaeangliae*). *Canadian Journal of Zoology* 66:1322–1327.

19. Zahavi, A. 1975. Mate selection—A selection for a handicap. *Journal of Theoretical Biology* 53(1):205–214.

20. Trivers, R.L. 1972. Parental investment and sexual selection. In B. Campbell, ed. *Sexual selection and the descent of man, 1871-1971*. Chicago: Aldine. Pages 136–179.

Notes to chapter 9

1. Darwin Correspondence Database, http://www.darwinproject. ac.uk/entry-2437 accessed on Fri Jul 31 2015. The Correspondence of Charles Darwin: 1858-1859 (vol-7). Burkhardt, F., and Smith, S. Cambridge University Press, 1992.

2. Darwin Correspondence Database, http://www.darwinproject. ac.uk/entry-2515 accessed on Fri Jul 31 2015. The Correspondence of Charles Darwin: 1858-1859 (vol-7). Burkhardt, F., and Smith, S. Cambridge University Press, 1992. Reproduced by permission from Cambridge University Press.

3. Darwin Correspondence Database, http://www.darwinproject. ac.uk/entry-2524 accessed on Fri Jul 31 2015. The Correspondence of Charles Darwin: 1858-1859 (vol-7). Burkhardt, F., and Smith, S. Cambridge University Press, 1992. Reproduced by permission from Cambridge University Press.

4. Darwin, C. R.1859. *On the origin of species by means of natural selection, or the preservation of favoured races in the struggle for life.* First edition. London: John Murray. First issue, page 84. In John van Wyhe, ed. 2002- *The Complete Work of Charles Darwin Online* (http://darwin-online.org.uk)

5. Darwin, C.R. 1859. *On the origin of species by means of natural selection, or the preservation of favoured races in the struggle for life.* First edition. London: John Murray. First issue, page 490. In John van Wyhe, ed. 2002- *The Complete Work of Charles Darwin Online* (http://darwin-online.org.uk)

6. Darwin Correspondence Database, http://www.darwinproject. ac.uk/entry-2575 accessed on Fri Jul 31 2015. The Correspondence of Charles Darwin: 1858-1859 (vol-7). Burkhardt, F., and Smith, S. Cambridge University Press, 1992. Reproduced by permission from Cambridge University Press.

7. Ibid.

8. Darwin Correspondence Database, http://www.darwinproject. ac.uk/entry-8449 accessed on Fri Jul 31 2015. The Correspondence of Charles Darwin: 1872 (vol-20). Burkhardt, F., Secord, J., and The Editors of The Darwin Correspondence Project. Cambridge University Press, 2013. Reproduced by permission from Cambridge University Press.

9. Darwin, C.R. 1859. *On the origin of species by means of natural selection, or the preservation of favoured races in the struggle for life.* First edition. London: John Murray. First issue, page 464. In John van Wyhe, ed. 2002- *The Complete Work of Charles Darwin Online* (http://darwin-online.org.uk)

10. Darwin Correspondence Database, http://www.darwin-project.ac.uk/entry-3899 accessed on Fri Jul 31 2015. The Correspondence of Charles Darwin: 1863 (vol-11). Burkhardt, F. et al. Cambridge University Press, 2000. Reproduced by permission from Cambridge University Press.

11. Woodward, Henry. 1874. New facts bearing on the inquiry concerning forms intermediate between birds and reptiles. *Quarterly Journal of the Geological Society*, 30:8–15. DOI:10.1144/ GSL.JGS.1874.030.01-04.16.

12. Clack, J.A. 2006. The emergence of early tetrapods. *Palaeogeography, Palaeoclimatology, Palaeoecology,* 232(2–4). Page 167–189.

13. Ahlberg, Per Erik and Clack, Jennifer A. 2006. Palaeontology: a firm step from water to land. *Nature* 440:747–749.

14. Flower, W.H. 1883. On whales, past and present, and their probable origin. *Nature* 28:226-230. DOI:10.1038/440747a.

15. Thewissen, J.G.M., Williams, E.M., Roe, L.J., and Hussain, S.T. 2001. Skeletons of terrestrial cetaceans and the relationship of whales to artiodactyls. *Nature* 413:277–281. DOI:10.1038/35095005.

16. Gatesy, J., Hayashi, C., Cronin, M.A., Arctander, P. 1996. Evidence from milk casein genes that cetaceans are close relatives of hippopotamid artiodactyls. *Molecular Biology and Evolution,* 13(7):954–963.

17. Darwin, C.R. 1859. *On the origin of species by means of natural selection, or the preservation of favoured races in the struggle for life.* First edition. London: John Murray. First issue, page 184. In John van Wyhe, ed. 2002- *The Complete Work of Charles Darwin Online* (http://darwin-online.org.uk)

18. Darwin Correspondence Database, http://www.darwin-project.ac.uk/entry-3071 accessed on Fri Jul 31 2015. The Correspondence of Charles Darwin: 1861 (vol-9). Burkhardt, F et al. Cambridge University Press, 1994. Reproduced by permission from Cambridge University Press.

Notes to chapter 10

1. Darwin, C.R. 1859. *On the origin of species by means of natural selection, or the preservation of favoured races in the struggle for life.* First edition. London: John Murray. First issue, page 488. In John van Wyhe, ed. 2002- *The Complete Work of Charles Darwin Online* (http://darwin-online.org.uk)

2. Darwin Correspondence Database, http://www.darwinproject. ac.uk/entry-2647 accessed on Fri Jul 31 2015. The Correspondence of Charles Darwin: 1860 (vol-8). Burkhardt, F. et al. Cambridge University Press, 1993. Reproduced by permission from Cambridge University Press.

3. Thomas Henry Huxley. 1863. *Evidence as to man's place in nature.* London: Williams & Norgate, 1863.

4. *Macmillan's Magazine.* October 1898.

5. Darwin Correspondence Database, http://www.darwinproject. ac.uk/entry-2852 accessed on Fri Jul 31 2015. The Correspondence of Charles Darwin: 1860 (vol-8). Burkhardt, F. et al. Cambridge University Press, 1993. Reproduced by permission from Cambridge University Press.

6. Darwin, C.R. 1871. *The descent of man, and selection in relation to sex.* Volume 1. London: John Murray. First edition, page201. In John van Wyhe, ed. 2002- *The Complete Work of Charles Darwin Online* (http://darwin-online.org.uk)

7. Darwin, C.R. 1871. *The descent of man, and selection in relation to sex.* Volume 1. London: John Murray. First edition, page 199. In

John van Wyhe, ed. 2002- *The Complete Work of Charles Darwin Online* (http://darwin-online.org.uk)

8. Dart, R.A. 1959. Adventures with the Missing Link. New York: Harper and Brothers.

9. Dart, R.A. 1925. Australopithecus africanus: The man-ape of South Africa. *Nature* 115:195–199. DOI: 10.1038/115195a0.

10. L.S.B.Leakey. 1959. A new fossil skull from Olduvai. *Nature* 184:491–493.

11. Johanson, D., Lovejoy, C.O., Kimbel, W.H., White, T.D., Ward, S.C., et al. 1982. Morphology of the Pliocene partial hominid skeleton (A.L. 288-1) from the Hadar formation, Ethiopia. *American Journal of Physical Anthropology* 57(4):403–451. DOI:10.1002/ajpa.1330570403.

12. Brunet, M., Guy, F., Pilbeam, D., Mackaye, H.T., Likius, A., et al. 2002. A new hominid from the Upper Miocene of Chad, Central Africa. *Nature* 418:145–151. DOI:10.1038/nature00879.

13. Thomas Henry Huxley. 1863. *Evidence as to man's place in nature*. London: Williams & Norgate.

Notes to chapter 11

1. Darwin, C.R. 1868. *The variation of animals and plants under domestication*. Volume 2. First edition, first issue. London: John Murray. Page 2. In John van Wyhe, ed. 2002- *The Complete Work of Charles Darwin Online* (http://darwin-online.org.uk)

2. Darwin Correspondence Database, http://www.darwinproject. ac.uk/entry-1352 accessed on Fri Jul 31 2015. The Correspondence of Charles Darwin: 1847-1850 (vol-4). Burkhardt, F., and Smith, S. Cambridge University Press, 1989. Reproduced by permission from Cambridge University Press.

3. Darwin Correspondence Database, http://www.darwin-project.ac.uk/entry-1476 accessed on Fri Jul 31 2015. The Correspondence of Charles Darwin: 1851-1855 (vol-5). Burkhardt, F., and Smith, S. Cambridge University Press, 1990. Reproduced by permission from Cambridge University Press.

4. Jenkin, F. 1867. On the origin of species. Review. *The North British Review* 46:277–318.

5. Ibid.

6. Mendel, Gregor. Experiments in Plant Hybridization. Paper read at meetings of the Brünn Natural History Society, February 8 and March 8, 1865. 1866. Versuche über Pflanzenhybriden. *Verhandlungen des naturforschenden Vereines in Brünn, Bd. IV für das Jahr 1865, Abhandlungen 3–47.* Translated by William Bateson in 1902.

7. Haldane, J.B.S. 1963. *Journal of Genetics*, 58(3) (December 1963), page 457.

8. Haldane, J.B.S. 1963. *Journal of Genetics*, 58(3) (December 1963), page 464.

9. Delisle, I. and Strobeck, C. 2005. A phylogeny of the Caniformia (order Carnivora) based on 12 complete protein-coding mitochondrial genes. *Molecular Phylogenetics and Evolution* 37:192-201.

Notes to chapter 12

1. Darwin Correspondence Database, http://www.darwinproject.ac.uk/entry-4004 accessed on Fri Jul 31 2015. The Correspondence of Charles Darwin: 1863 (vol-11). Burkhardt, F et al. Cambridge University Press, 2000. Reproduced by permission from Cambridge University Press.

2. Darwin Correspondence Database, http://www.darwinproject.ac.uk/entry-3356 accessed on Fri Jul 31 2015. The Correspondence of Charles Darwin: 1862 (vol-10). Burkhardt, F. et al. Cambridge: Cambridge University Press, 1997. Reproduced by permission from Cambridge University Press.

3. Darwin Correspondence Database, http://www.darwinproject.ac.uk/entry-3411 accessed on Fri Jul 31 2015. The Correspondence of Charles Darwin: 1862 (vol-10). Burkhardt, F. et al. Cambridge: Cambridge University Press, 1997. Reproduced by permission from Cambridge University Press.

4. Wallace, A.R. 1895. *Natural selection and tropical nature: Essays on descriptive and theoretical biology*. London: Macmillan.

5. Muchhala, N. 2006. Nectar bat stows huge tongue in rib cage. *Nature* 444:701–702.

6. O'Brien, S.J. et al. 1985. Genetic basis for species vulnerability in the cheetah. *Science* 227(4693):1428–1434. DOI: 10.1126/science.2983425.

7. Menotti-Raymond, M.A and O'Brien, S.J. 1993. Dating the genetic bottleneck of the African cheetah. *Proceedings of the National Academy of Sciences U S A* 90:3172–3176.

8. Ritland, K., Newton, C., Marshall, H.D. 2001. Inheritance and population structure of the white-phased "Kermode" black bear. *Current Biology* 11(18):1468–1472.

9. Hoelzel R.A. and Dover, G.A. 1991. Genetic differentiation between sympatric killer whale populations. *Heredity* 66:191–195. DOI:10.1038/hdy.1991.24.

10. Byrne, K. and Nichols, R.A. 1999. *Culex pipiens* in London Underground tunnels: differentiation between surface and subterranean populations. *Heredity* 82:7–15.

11. Gentile, G., et al. 2009. An overlooked pink species of land iguana in the Galápagos. *Proceedings of the National Academy of Sciences U S A*. DOI: 10.1073/pnas.0806339106.

Notes to chapter 13

1. Darrow, Clarence and William J. Bryan. The World's Most Famous Court Trial. Tennessee Evolution Case. A Complete Stenographic Report of the Famous Court Test of the Anti-Evolution Act, at Dayton July 10 to 21, 1925, Including Speeches and Arguments of Attorneys. Originally published:

   Cincinnati: National Book Company, [1925]. Reprinted 1997, 2010 by The Lawbook Exchange, Ltd.

   Excerpts of testimonials from the trial can also be found on http://www.law.umkc.edu/faculty/projects/FTrials/scopes/scopes.htm.

2. Epperson v. Arkansas 393 U.S. 97 (1968). U.S. Supreme Court ruling. November 12, 1968.

3. Edwards v. Aguillard 482 U.S. 578 (1987). U.S. Supreme Court ruling. June 19, 1987.

4. Kitzmiller v. Dover Area School District. 2005. U.S. District Court for the Middle District of Pennsylvania. Docket number 4cv2688.

5. Miller, J.D., Scott, E.C., and Okamoto, S. 2006. Public acceptance of evolution. *Science* 313(5788):765–766. DOI:10.1126/science.1126746.

6. Committee on Culture, Science and Education, Parliamentary Assembly of the Council of Europe. 2007. The dangers of creationism in education. (Resolution 1580: October 4, 2007.

7. Blancke, Stefaan, Hjermitslev, Hans Henrik, and Kjærgaard, Peter C. eds. 2014. *Creationism in Europe*. Baltimore: Johns Hopkins University Press.

8. Darwin, C.R. 1958. *The autobiography of Charles Darwin 1809–1882. With the original omissions restored. Edited and with appendix and notes by his grand-daughter Nora Barlow.* London: Collins. Page 85. In John van Wyhe, ed. 2002- *The Complete Work of Charles Darwin Online* (http://darwin-online.org.uk)

9. Darwin, C.R. 1958. *The autobiography of Charles Darwin 1809–1882. With the original omissions restored. Edited and with appendix and notes by his grand-daughter Nora Barlow.* London:

Collins. Page 87. In John van Wyhe, ed. 2002- *The Complete Work of Charles Darwin Online* (http://darwin-online.org.uk)

10. Darwin Correspondence Database, http://www.darwin-project.ac.uk/entry-2855 accessed on Sat Aug 8 2015. The Correspondence of Charles Darwin: 1860 (vol-8). Burkhardt, F. et al. Cambridge University Press, 1993. Reproduced by permission from Cambridge University Press.

11. Darwin Correspondence Database, http://www.darwin-project.ac.uk/entry-2814 accessed on Sat Aug 8 2015. The Correspondence of Charles Darwin: 1860 (vol-8). Burkhardt, F. et al. Cambridge University Press, 1993. Reproduced by permission from Cambridge University Press.

12. Darwin Correspondence Database, http://www.darwinproject. ac.uk/entry-761 accessed on Fri Aug 7 2015. The Correspondence of Charles Darwin: 1844-1846 (vol-3). Burkhardt, F., and Smith, S. Cambridge University Press, 1988. Reproduced by permission from Cambridge University Press.

13. Darwin, C.R. 1958. *The autobiography of Charles Darwin 1809–1882. With the original omissions restored. Edited and with appendix and notes by his grand-daughter Nora Barlow.* London: Collins. Pages 140–145. In John van Wyhe, ed. 2002- *The Complete Work of Charles Darwin Online* (http://darwin-online.org.uk)

14. Darwin Correspondence Database, http://www.darwinproject.ac.uk/entry-13682 accessed on Sat Aug 8 2015.

15. Darwin, Francis ed. 1887. *The life and letters of Charles Darwin, including an autobiographical chapter.* Volume 3. London: John Murray. Page 358. In John van Wyhe, ed. 2002- *The Complete Work of Charles Darwin Online* (http://darwin-online.org.uk)

16. Darwin, C.R. 1871. *The descent of man, and selection in relation to sex.* Volume 1, first edition. London: John Murray. Page 3. In John van Wyhe, ed. 2002- *The Complete Work of Charles Darwin Online* (http://darwin-online.org.uk)

Bibliography

The bibliography contains the books, letters, articles, diaries, and other manuscripts cited in this book as well as those used in research for the book. The abbreviation CUL-DAR refers to Cambridge University Library - Darwin Archive.

Alvarez, Walter. 1997. *T. rex and the Crater of Doom*. Princeton University Press

Alvarez LW, Alvarez W, Asaro F, and Michel HV. 1980. Extraterrestrial cause for the Cretaceous-Tertiary extinction. *Science* 208 (4448): 1095–1108

Barlow, Nora (Ed.). 1958. *The autobiography of Charles Darwin 1809–1882. With the original omissions restored. Edited and with appendix and notes by his grand-daughter Nora Barlow*. London: Collins. In John van Wyhe, ed. 2002- *The Complete Work of Charles Darwin Online* (http://darwin-online.org.uk)

Barlow, Nora (Ed.). 1963. Darwin's ornithological notes. *Bulletin of the British Museum (Natural History)*. Historical Series (2:7):201–278. With introduction, notes, and appendix by the editor. In John van Wyhe, ed. 2002- *The Complete Work of Charles Darwin Online* (http://darwin-online.org.uk)

Beale, Thomas. 1839. *The Natural History of the Sperm Whale*. London, Van Voorst

Bowler, Peter. 1989. *Evolution: The History of an Idea* (revised edition). California: University of California Press

Browne, Janet. 1995. *Charles Darwin: Voyaging.* Volume 1. New York: Alfred Knopf Inc; London: Jonathan Cape Ltd

Browne, Janet. 2002. *Charles Darwin: The Power of Place.* Volume 2. New York: Alfred Knopf Inc.; London: Jonathan Cape Ltd

Brunet M *et al.* 2002. A new hominid from the Upper Miocene of Chad, Central Africa. *Nature* 418(6894):145–151

Burness, Gary P, Jared Diamond, and Timothy Flannery. 2001. Dinosaurs, dragons, and dwarfs: The evolution of maximal body size. *Proceedings of the National Academy of Sciences* 98(25):14518–14523

Byrne, K and RA Nichols. 1999. *Culex pipiens* in London Underground tunnels: differentiation between surface and subterranean populations. *Heredity* 82:7–15

Chu, KC. 1988. Dive times and ventilation patterns of singing humpback whales (*Megaptera novaeangliae*). *Canadian Journal of Zoology* **66**:1322–1327

Clack, JA. 2006. The emergence of early tetrapods. *Palaeogeography, Palaeoclimatology, Palaeoecology* 232(2–4):167–189

Committee on Culture, Science and Education (Parliamentary Assembly, Council of Europe). *The dangers of creationism in education.* Doc. 11297. June 8, 2007. Reported by Guy Lengagne, France, Socialist Group

Dart RA. 1925. *Australopithecus africanus*: The man-ape of South Africa. *Nature* 115:195–199

Dart, RA. 1959. *Adventures with the Missing Link.* 1959. New York: Harper

Darwin, CR. Beagle animal notes (1832–1833)] CUL-DAR29.1.A1– A49. In John van Wyhe, ed. 2002- *The Complete Work of Charles Darwin Online* (http://darwin-online.org.uk)

Darwin, CR. *The Zoology of the Voyage of H.M.S. Beagle, under the Command of Captain FitzRoy, R.N., during the Years 1832 to 1836. Part I. Fossil Mammalia. By Richard Owen, ESQ. F.R.S. Professor of Anatomy and Physiology to The Royal College of Surgeons In London; Corresponding member of the Institute of France. Published with the approval of the Lords Commissioners of Her Majesty's Treasury. Edited and superintended by Charles Darwin, ESQ. M.A. F.R.S. SEC. G.S. Naturalist to the expedition.* In John van Wyhe, ed. 2002- *The Complete Work of Charles Darwin Online* (http:// darwin-online.org.uk)

Darwin, CR. *Notebook B: Transmutation of species* (1837–1838). CUL-DAR121. . In John van Wyhe, ed. 2002- *The Complete Work of Charles Darwin Online* (http://darwin-online.org.uk)

Darwin, CR. 1839. *Narrative of the Surveying Voyages of His Majesty's Ships Adventure and Beagle between the Years 1826 and 1836, Describing their Examination of the Southern Shores of South America, and the Beagle's Circumnavigation of the Globe. Journal and Remarks. 1832–1836.* London: Henry Colburn. In John van Wyhe, ed. 2002- *The Complete Work of Charles Darwin Online* (http://darwin-online.org.uk)

Darwin, CR. 1845. *Journal of Researches into the Natural History and Geology of the Countries Visited during the Voyage of H.M.S.*

Beagle round the World, under the Command of Capt. FitzRoy, R.N. Second edition. London: John Murray. In John van Wyhe, ed. 2002- *The Complete Work of Charles Darwin Online* (http://darwin-online.org.uk)

Darwin, CR. 1859. *On the Origin of Species by Means of Natural Selection, or the Preservation of Favoured Races in the Struggle for Life. By Charles Darwin, M.A.* London: John Murray, Albemarle Street. In John van Wyhe, ed. 2002- *The Complete Work of Charles Darwin Online* (http://darwin-online.org.uk)

Darwin, CR. 1868. *The Variation of Animals and Plants under Domestication.* First edition, first issue. Volume 2. London: John Murray. In John van Wyhe, ed. 2002- *The Complete Work of Charles Darwin Online* (http://darwin-online.org.uk)

Darwin, CR. 1871. *The Descent of Man, and Selection in Relation to Sex.* First edition. London: John Murray. In John van Wyhe, ed. 2002- *The Complete Work of Charles Darwin Online* (http://darwin-online.org.uk)

Darwin, CR. Shot (Notes on shooting). CUL-DAR91.1. In John van Wyhe, ed. 2002- *The Complete Work of Charles Darwin Online* (http://darwin-online.org.uk)

Darwin, Francis (Ed.). 1887. *The Life and Letters of Charles Darwin, Including an Autobiographical Chapter.* Volumes 1 and 2. London: John Murray. In John van Wyhe, ed. 2002- *The Complete Work of Charles Darwin Online* (http://darwin-online.org.uk)

Dawkins, Richard. 1986. *The Blind Watchmaker.* New York: W.W. Norton & Company

Dawkins, Richard. 1989. *The Selfish Gene.* Second edition. Oxford: Oxford University Press

Dawkins, Richard. 1996. *Climbing Mount Improbable.* New York: W.W. Norton & Company

Delisle I and Strobeck, C. 2005. A phylogeny of the Caniformia (order Carnivora) based on 12 complete protein-coding mitochondrial genes. *Molecular Phylogenetics and Evolution* 37:192–201

Dennett, Daniel. 1995. *Darwin's Dangerous Idea.* New York: Simon & Schuster

Desmond, Adrian and Moore, James. 1992. *Darwin.* London: Michael Joseph, Penguin Group

Diamond, Jared. 1992. *The Third Chimpanzee : The Evolution and Future of the Human Animal.* New York : HarperCollins Publishers

Edwards v. Aguillard. 1987. Case number 482 U.S. 578 in the Supreme Court of the United States. June 19, 1987

Eldredge N. 2005. *Darwin: Discovering the Tree of Life.* W.W. Norton & Company, New York

Emslie SD and William P. Patterson. 2007. Abrupt recent shift in $\delta^{13}C$ and $\delta^{15}N$ values in Adélie penguin eggshell in Antarctica. *PNAS 2007 104: 11666–11669.*

Enattah NS, Sahi T, Savilahti E, Terwilliger JD et al. 2002. Identification of a variant associated with adult-type hypolactasia. *Nature Genetics* 30:233–237

Epperson v. Arkansas. 1968. 393 U.S. 97 (1968). November 12, 1968

FitzRoy, R. 1839. *Narrative of the Surveying Voyages of His Majesty's Ships Adventure and Beagle between the Years 1826 and 1836, Describing their Examination of the Southern Shores of South America, and the Beagle's Circumnavigation of the Globe. Proceedings of the Second Expedition, 1831–36, under the Command of Captain Robert Fitz-Roy, R.N.* London: Henry Colburn. In John van Wyhe, ed. 2002- *The Complete Work of Charles Darwin Online* (http://darwin-online.org.uk)

Flower WH. 1883. On Whales, Past and Present, and their Probable Origin. *Nature* 28:199–202 and 226–230

Gatesy J, Hayashi C, Cronin MA, Arctander P. 1996. Evidence from milk casein genes that cetaceans are close relatives of hippopotamid artiodactyls. *Molecular Biology and Evolution* 13(7):954–63

Gentile G. et al. 2009. An overlooked pink species of land iguana in the Galápagos. *Proceedings of the National Academy of Sciences* doi:0806339106

Haldane JBS. 1963. *Journal of Genetics* 58(3). Book reviews

Haupt, Lyanda L. 2006. *Pilgrim on the Great Bird Continent, the Importance of Everything and Other Lessons from Darwin's Lost Notebooks.* New York: Little, Brown

Herbert, Sandra. 2005. *Charles Darwin, Geologist.* Ithaca/New York/London: Cornell University Press

Hoelzel RA and Gabriel A. Dover. 1991. Genetic differentiation between sympatric killer whale populations. *Heredity* 66:191–195; doi:10.1038/hdy.1991.24

Holten, Birgitte and Michael Sterll. 1998. Et genfundet brev: Naturforskeren P.W. Lunds afsluttende rapport fra udgravningerne ved Lagoa Santa. *Fund og Forskning 37*

Huxley, Thomas Henry. 1863. *Evidence as to Man's Place in Nature.* Williams & Norgate

Jenkin F. 1867. On the Origin of Species. Review. *The North British Review* 46:277–318

Johanson D, CO Lovejoy, WH Kimbel, TD White et al. 1982. Morphology of the Pliocene partial hominid skeleton (AL 288-1) from the Hadar Formation, Ethiopia. *American Journal of Physical Anthropology* 57:403–451

Jukema J and T Piersma. 2006. Permanent female mimics in a lekking shorebird. Biology Letters 2(2):161–164

Kettlewell HBD. 1955. Selection experiments on industrial melanism in the Lepidoptera. *Heredity* 9:323–342

Kettlewell HBD. 1956. Further selection experiments on industrial melanism in the Lepidoptera. *Heredity* 10:287–301

Keynes, Richard (Ed.) 2000. *Charles Darwin's Zoology Notes & Specimen Lists from H.M.S. Beagle.* Cambridge: Cambridge University Press. In John van Wyhe, ed. 2002- *The Complete Work of Charles Darwin Online* (http://darwin-online.org.uk)

Keynes, Richard (Ed.) 2001. *Charles Darwin's Beagle Diary.* Cambridge: Cambridge University Press. In John van Wyhe, ed. 2002- *The Complete Work of Charles Darwin Online* (http://darwin-online.org.uk)

Keynes, Randal. 2001. *Annie's Box: Charles Darwin, His Daughter and Human Evolution.* London: Fourth Estate. In John van Wyhe, ed. 2002- *The Complete Work of Charles Darwin Online* (http://darwin-online.org.uk)

Kitzmiller *v.* Dover Area School District. Case number 4:04-CV-02688 in the United States District Court for the Middle District of Pennsylvania

Kristensen M, M Knorr, AM Rasmussen, and JB Jespersen. 2006. Survey of permethrin and malathion resistance in human head lice populations from Denmark. *Journal of Medical Entomology* 43(3):533–538

Leakey, LSB. 1959. A new fossil skull from Olduvai. *Nature* 184:491–493

Leakey, Richard. 1994. *The Origin of Humankind.* New York: Perseus Books Group

Leboeuf BJ and S Mesnick. 1991. Sexual behavior of male northern elephant seals. I: Lethal injuries to adult females. *Behaviour* 116(1–2):143–162

Linnaeus C. 1729. *Præludia Sponsaliorum Plantarum*

Litchfield HE (Ed.) 1915. *Emma Darwin: A Century of Family Letters, 1792–1896.* Volume 2. London: John Murray. In John van Wyhe, ed. 2002- *The Complete Work of Charles Darwin Online* (http://darwin-online.org.uk)

Lund PW. 1836. *Om Huler i Kalksteen i det Indre af Brasilien, der Tildeels Indeholde Fossile Knokler.* Første afhandling. Særskilt Aftryk af det Kongelige Danske Videnskabernes Selskabs skrifter

Lyell, Charles. 1853. *Principles of Geology, Being an Attempt to Explain the Former Changes of the Earth's Surface, by Reference to Causes Now in Operation.* Volume 1. London: John Murray

Macmillan's Magazine. October 1898

Majerus MEN. 1998. *Melanism: Evolution in Action.* Oxford University Press

Malthus, Thomas. 1798. *An Essay on the Principle of Population, as it Affects the Future Improvement of Society with Remarks on the Speculations of Mr. Godwin, M. Condorcet, and Other Writers. LONDON, PRINTED FOR J. JOHNSON, IN ST. PAUL'S CHURCH-YARD*

Marchant, James. 1916. *Alfred Russel Wallace: Letters and Reminiscences.* New York: Harper & Brothers

Maynard Smith, John. 1988. *Did Darwin Get It Right? Essays on Games, Sex and Evolution.* London: Chapman & Hall

Mayr, Ernst. 1942. *Systematics and the Origin of Species, from the Viewpoint of a Zoologist.* Cambridge: Harvard University Press

Mayr, Ernst. 2000. *What Evolution Is.* New York: Basic Books

Mendel, Gregor. 1865. *Versuche über Pflanzenhybriden.* Verhandlungen des naturforschenden Vereins in Brünn, IV. Band. Abhandlungen 1865, Brünn. 1866. Commentary by William Bateson in 1902. Im Verlage des Vereins. Pages 3–47

Menotti-Raymond MA and SJ O'Brien. 1993. Dating the genetic bottleneck of the African cheetah. *Proceedings of the National Academy of Sciences* 90:3172–3176

Millien V. 2006. Morphological evolution is accelerated among island mammals. *PLoS Biology* 4(11):e384

Muchhala N. 2006. Nectar bat stows huge tongue in rib cage. *Nature* 444:701–702

Myers N, RA Mittermeier, CG Mittermeier, GAB Fonseca et al. 2000. Biodiversity hotspots for conservation priorities. *Nature.* 403:853–858

New Scientist. April 5, 2006. First fossil of fish that crawled onto land discovered

O'Brien SJ, ME Roelke, L Marker, A Newman et al. 1985. Genetic basis for species vulnerability in the cheetah. *Science* 227:1428–1434

Owen, Richard. 1894. *The Life of Richard Owen by His Grandson Richard Owen*. Two volumes. London: J. Murray

Paley, William. 1802. *Natural Theology*. London: J. Faulder

Prideaux GJ, RG Roberts, D Megirian, KE Westaway et al. 2007. Mammalian responses to Pleistocene climate change in southeastern Australia. *Geology* 35(1):33–36

Quammen, David. 1996. *The Song of the Dodo: Island Biogeography in an Age of Extinctions*. New York: Scribner

Quammen, David. 2006. *The Reluctant Mr. Darwin: An Intimate Portrait of Charles Darwin and the Making of His Theory of Evolution*. W. W. Norton

Ritland K, C Newton, and H Marshall. 2001. Inheritance and population structure of the white-phased "Kermode" black bear. *Current Biology* 11(18):1468–1472

Roca, Alfred L, Nicholas Georgiadis, Jill Pecon-Slattery, and Stephen J. OBrien. 2001. Genetic Evidence for Two Species of Elephant in Africa. *Science* 293(5534):1473–1477

Rosing M, DK Bird, NH Sleep, W Glassley et al. F. 2006. The rise of continents—An essay on the geologic consequences of photosynthesis. *Palaeogegraphy, Palaeoclimatology, Palaeoecology* 232:99–113

Roth LV. 1992. Inferences from allometry and fossils: Dwarfing of elephants on islands. *Oxford Surveys in Evolutionary Biology* 8: 259–288

Schmitz, Birger, David AT Harper, Bernhard Peucker-Ehrenbrink, Svend Stouge et al. 2008. Asteroid breakup linked to the Great Ordovician Biodiversification Event. *Nature Geoscience* 1:49–53

Scopes, John Thomas and William Jennings Bryan. 1925. *The World's Most Famous Court Trial, Tennessee Evolution Case; A Complete Stenographic Report of the Famous Court Test of the Tennessee Anti-Evolution Act, at Dayton, July 10 to 21, 1925, Including Speeches and Arguments of Attorneys.* Originally published:

Cincinnati: National Book Company, [1925]. Reprinted 1997, 2010 by The Lawbook Exchange, Ltd.

Stott, Rebecca. 2003. *Darwin and the Barnacle: The Story of One Tiny Creature and History's Most Spectacular Scientific Breakthrough.* New York: W.W. Norton & Company

Sulloway FJ. 1982. The Beagle collections of Darwin's finches (Geospizinae). *Bulletin of the British Museum (Natural History) Historical Series* 43(2):49–94. In John van Wyhe, ed. 2002- *The Complete Work of Charles Darwin Online* (http://darwin-online. org.uk)

Thewissen JGM, EM Williams, LJ Roe, and ST Hussain. 2001. Skeletons of terrestrial cetaceans and the relationship of whales to artiodactyls. *Nature* 413:277–281

Tishkoff SA, FA Reed, A Ranciaro, BF Voight et al. 2006. Convergent adaptation of human lactase persistence in Africa and Europe. *Nature Genetics* **39**:31–40

Trivers RL. 1972. Parental investment and sexual selection. In Campbell, BG (Ed.). *Sexual Selection and the Descent of Man.* 1972. Chicago: Aldine. Pages 136–179

Wallace, Alfred Russel. 1855. On the Law Which Has Regulated the Introduction of New Species [dated Feb. 1855, Sarawak, Borneo]. *Annals and Magazine of Natural History* 16 (second series): 184–196. September 1855

Wallace, Alfred Russel. 1895. *Natural Selection and Tropical Nature: Essays on Descriptive and Theoretical Biology.* London: Macmillan

Wallace, Alfred Russel, 1905. *My Life: A Record of Events and Opinions.* London: Chapman and Hall

Woodward, Henry. 1874. New facts bearing on the inquiry concerning forms intermediate between birds and reptiles. *Quarterly Journal of the Geological Society*

Wyhe, John van ed. 2002- The Complete Work of Charles Darwin Online (http://darwin-online.org.uk)

Zahavi A. 1975. Mate selection—a selection for a handicap. *Journal of Theoretical Biology* 53:205—214

Zahavi A. and A Zahavi. 1997. *The Handicap Principle: A Missing Piece of Darwin's Puzzle.* Oxford: Oxford University Press

Zimmer, Carl. 2001. *Evolution: The Triumph of an Idea.* New York: HarperCollins Publishers

Made in the USA
Middletown, DE
30 November 2018

The story of Darwin's life
and how his ideas
changed everything

Part biography, part popular science,
A Modest Genius provides a lively,
engaging account of Darwin's life and the
events that inspired his groundbreaking
theory. Science writer and biologist Hanne
Strager brings Darwin to life while offering
the essential elements of evolution and how
they affect us today.

Bold, exciting, and easily understood,
A Modest Genius offers an opportunity to
understand one of the greatest scientific
breakthroughs of the modern age.

Hanne Strager

Hailing from Denmark, Hanne Strager is a biologist and
science writer. After receiving an education from the
University Aarhus, Denmark, she studied at the University
of California, Santa Cruz, as a Fulbright Scholar.

ISBN 9781517714338

90000 >

9 781517 714338